BUILDING BRANDS WITH WITH SOUL

"Nothing more critical for marketing leader than crafting and amplifying a brand's soul. This book will help you navigate the ins and outs of this fascinating and fulfilling experience."

— **Cristina Bondolowoski**
Global CMO of MSCI

"A refreshingly human approach to an increasingly de-humanised brand strategy process, packed full of useful anecdotes and practical tips drawn from extensive lived experiences with highly successful global brands. Aspiring leaders, along with established CEOs or CMOs looking to reconnect with meaning and purpose in their role and output should take note of this book, which is a timely reminder that empathy is the most powerful tool we have."

— **Tim Parkinson**
Former CMO and SVP at Nike Inc.,
Under Armour, Diageo and Wieden + Kennedy

"Siew Ting's book offers advice that is both timeless and perfect for the current crossroads that marketers find themselves in. She shares her reflections on building brands with humanity and soul at their core, and also reflects on her own journey to becoming a soulful leader and marketer. As Siew Ting reflects on her journey across continents, brands and marketing practices, she also encourages readers to reflect on themselves and their current situations. I've found myself thinking about how to lead with soul and cut to the heart of what matters, long after putting down this book!"

— **Philip Ryan**
Managing Partner at Ipsos Strategy3

BUILDING BRANDS WITH SOUL

A CMO's Journey to Humanising Growth
and Creating Meaningful Impact

Foo Siew Ting

Candid Creation Publishing

First published 2024

Candid Creation Publishing books are available through most major bookstores in Singapore. For bulk order of our books at special quantity discounts, please email us at enquiry@candidcreation.com.

BUILDING BRANDS WITH SOUL
A CMO's Journey to Humanising Growth and Creating Meaningful Impact

Author: Foo Siew Ting
Publisher: Phoon Kok Hwa
Editor: Zoe Toh
Page Layout: Geelyn Lim
Cover Design: Ryanne Ng
Published by: Candid Creation Publishing LLP
               167 Jalan Bukit Merah
               #05-12 Connection One Tower 4
               Singapore 150167
Website: www.candidcreation.com
Email: enquiry@candidcreation.com
Facebook: www.facebook.com/CandidCreationPublishing
ISBN: 978-981-17560-5-4

National Library Board, Singapore Cataloguing in Publication Data
Name(s): Foo, Siew Ting.
Title: Building brands with soul : a CMO's journey to humanising growth and creating meaningful impact / Foo Siew Ting.
Description: Singapore : Candid Creation Publishing LLP, 2024.
Identifier(s): ISBN 978-981-17560-5-4 (paperback)
Subject(s): LCSH: Brand name products. | Branding (Marketing)--Management. | Foo, Siew Ting.
Classification: DDC 658.827--dc23

*In memory of my beloved mother who brought me up
to become who I am and who helped me
found my own voice.*

*To my family—Hon Fai, Kayla, Dad, and my two
sisters and their families—I love you with
my whole heart.*

*To the people and teams I have led in every step
of the last 25+ years—without you, I would not be
writing this book.*

Contents

Foreword

Building Brands with Soul, more than anything, is a story of a personal growth journey that has also manifested itself in business growth.

Siew Ting is an accomplished industry veteran. She has done all aspiring marketing leaders a huge favour by sharing her insights and knowledge from her own experiences at marketing powerhouses, such as Diageo, Unilever and Mars Inc..

As she makes it very clear, building brands with soul is not an easy feat. It requires a deep connection with your personal passion and purpose, as well as true grit, to manage all the internal stakeholders to ultimately create value for all parties involved, including the society and our planet. But Siew Ting also, in her own compelling and eloquent style, let us feel how rewarding and fulfilling this quest can be.

The source of Siew Ting's passion and perseverance can be found in her *ikigai*. It is the sweet spot between what you love, what you're good at, what you get paid for and what the world needs from you.

For Siew Ting, the concept of humanising growth—creating value for all stakeholders—is very much at the ikigai sweet spot.

Building an insightful understanding of the needs of all stakeholders is indeed quite a challenge. Creating value propositions that deliver against unmet needs for all stakeholders is even more difficult. This is where it gets interesting for marketers because now we are talking about the fundamental capabilities of the marketing function. This is where chief marketing officers (CMO) can help their CEOs and other C-suite colleagues deliver a more humanised growth strategy. This transition is creating a unique opportunity to increase influence. It is not just about re-establishing relevance and securing a future career path. Today's existential sustainability and social issues represent an urgent call to action for marketers to step up and take responsibility for helping their companies succeed and do the right thing.

The good news is that we are indeed seeing an increasing number of marketers do precisely that—collaborating with peers and partners to help the company drive more humanised growth. These CMOs are not only helping their businesses grow, but also using their power to influence consumer behaviour to create real, sustainable change.

Dove building brand growth and women's self-esteem, First Direct offering financial services and improving people's mental well-being, and Tide getting rid of stains and convincing consumers to wash at 30 degrees instead of 60 degrees. Now is the time for marketers to help achieve what former Unilever

CEO Paul Polman calls "the Business Plan for the Planet"—i.e., the United Nation's (UN) 17 Sustainable Development Goals (SDGs). As a marketer, you have the right experience, skills, capabilities and attitudes to get this done.

An important Institute for Real Growth (IRG) study on value creation found that businesses are indeed shifting their focus. Seventy-eight per cent of leaders in IRG's Humanised Growth Leadership Programme agreed that their business has evolved towards a more humanised growth strategy and 65 per cent of the participants reported that their influence on the business strategy has increased. This brings me back to the ikigai of marketing. The past years have caused massive disruption for people, businesses and marketers. It is this disruption that has created a situation where what the world needs fully correlates with what marketers can offer.

Stepping up to this responsibility is paying off morally and is being rewarded financially. More than 80 per cent of the Environmental, Social and Governance (ESG) funds outperformed their benchmarks. Moreover, meeting the UN's SDGs will unlock trillions in value and create hundreds of millions of jobs just in this decade alone. Therefore, the opportunity is to shift the focus from losing influence as marketers to stepping up and taking responsibility.

Building Brands with Soul provides marketers who do want to step up and regain influence by driving a humanised growth agenda with practical tools, frameworks, insights and lessons learnt.

Hopefully, this book will also be received as a call to action, action the world badly needs, because think of it: If not now, then when? And if not you, then who?

Frank van den Driest
Founder, Institute for Real Growth

Preface

In her timeless quote, Annie Dillard reminds us that "anything you do not give freely and abundantly becomes lost to you; you open your safe and find ashes".

This profound statement underpins the philosophy that has guided my career in marketing for more than 25 years—a journey that began shortly after I graduated from university, fuelled by a fortuitous internship and shaped by myriad experiences at some of the world's leading corporations.

In *Building Brands with Soul*, I aim to distil the essence of what I have learnt and practised as a marketing leader dedicated to cultivating brands that resonate deeply within their markets and society. This book is designed to serve as a robust guide for those aspiring to ascend to the role of a CMO, offering a blueprint that I wish had been available to me when I embarked on this exhilarating and challenging career path myself.

My Journey: From Intern to Marketing Leader

My adventure in marketing began with an eye-opening three-month internship at Scott Paper, which has since become part of Kimberly-Clark. This early experience was pivotal; I was mentored by three remarkable marketing leaders who designed an exceptional programme that immersed me in the craft of marketing. Their mentorship ignited my passion for this field, leading me to pursue a career in marketing under the graduate traineeship programme at Unilever.

Throughout my tenures at Unilever, Mars Inc. (hereafter "Mars") and Diageo, I have had the privilege of working under the guidance of numerous mentors and sponsors. These individuals ranged from successful entrepreneurs and creative officers to presidents and CEOs. Each of them provided me with invaluable insights and skills that refined my marketing abilities. More importantly, they recognised and nurtured my potential, took a chance on me, and empowered me to reach greater heights.

The Essence of the Book: Building Brands with Soul

The core of this book revolves around the concept of building brands and businesses with soul, as envisioned through the lens of a "purposeful CMO". It encapsulates a human-centric approach to the self, team and business leadership, emphasising on the necessity of a purposeful and inspiring vision. The modern business environment, characterised by turbulence and rapid change, demands a new breed of leadership—one that can engender trust, respect and empathy. This book offers actionable tips derived from my personal experiences, successes and failures, providing practical advice for navigating the complexities of contemporary marketing leadership.

Humanising Growth: My Interpretation

This book explores my personal interpretation of humanising growth, emphasising the need for comprehensive management of personal and team leadership to drive business success. It recounts the challenges and victories I have faced while building brands that resonate with both global and local audiences. Each chapter aims to provide mid-level marketers with the insights and tools necessary to advance towards their goal of becoming a CMO.

The Significance of "Soul" in Branding

The concept of soul resonates with me deeply. In a corporate sense, it captures the essence of all that is intangible within the business sphere. It is akin to the spirit of an entity, representing the deeper, often unquantifiable elements of a brand. In the realm of corporate leadership, particularly for those of us who navigate the challenging waters of the C-suite as CMOs, the soul of a brand plays a critical role in shaping our strategies and outcomes. While we engage with the tangible aspects of profit and loss statements, the value of a brand is vital too, as recent studies among Standard and Poor's (S&P) 500 companies have highlighted. These intangible assets are crucial not only for enhancing shareholder value, but also for securing a competitive edge in the global marketplace.

Being a CMO involves much more than managing the visible, glamorous aspects of the role. Beyond the external power and allure lies the intricate challenge of fostering business growth and crafting value through brands that embody soul, thereby making a significant and meaningful impact on the world. This task requires a masterful blend of personal leadership, self-awareness and team direction. It is an art form, as much as it is a scientific endeavour, reliant on a deep understanding of data-driven insights meshed with creative intuition.

This role demands a nuanced approach to balancing the quantitative with the qualitative, the empirical with the emotional. Building a brand with soul is about more than achieving financial growth. It involves influencing and impacting multiple stakeholders in a way that transcends traditional metrics. Through this process, we can deliver a brand's most important intangible assets effectively and resonantly.

Therefore, I use the term "soul" to describe the beating heart of my professional journey and the legacy I aim to leave behind. A brand with soul not only enhances the bottom line and growth, but also creates a rippling, positive impact that echoes through the lives of customers, employees and society at large. This, to me, is the essence of a soulful legacy, a legacy that leverages the power of intangible assets to forge enduring connections and build a world that is enriched by meaningful brands.

* * *

In the first 20 years of my career, I was very fortunate to have met different mentors who ultimately became the sponsors of my professional achievements. I was trained by the best entrepreneur, the world-class creative maverick, the best CMO and the best regional president. Each one of them helped me propel my career. They saw the potential in me and created the right opportunities, assignments and projects that helped me fast-track my potential even further.

As I reflect on these mentors throughout my career, I realise that my growth mindset has an innate importance. I was naturally very curious, hungry for knowledge and had a huge growth mindset—to want to learn from them and master each of the assignments.

I have been mentoring and coaching many of my team members over the last 10 years. Because I have a gift for identifying potential and guiding teams towards where this potential can be unleashed, I end up getting a lot of requests from people to help guide them. I also feel that the art, heart, and soul side of marketing is getting lost amid the current AI-cluttered world. The world we live in now is turbulent and, changes and transformations have become part and parcel of life.

Technology will get faster. It will commoditise brands, but humanity is the way to differentiate brands.

If you look at what marketing is all about, defined in its own rudimentary term, it is all about understanding the human minds, needs and motivations to create brands, products, solutions and services that best meet these needs. The world we live in now is messy. In this post-Covid "reset" world with the AI transformation, the future of work is changing fast. Organisational hierarchies are breaking down. Processes are constantly being reinvented by machines. Workstyle and workspace will have to evolve. The generation of young consumers seek purposeful and meaningful brands. They buy into the authenticity of brands. Hence, the soul of the brand and a human-centric approach are essential. It requires a different take on how leaders should lead into the future and what the brands and businesses will require to create a differentiating impact in the world.

I also believe in sharing my knowledge, as the world we live in now is going towards a sharing economy. By sharing more, you will learn more and become more enriched.

Hence, this book.

Building Brands with Soul is a simple guide that captures my perspective, formed on the basis of my professional experience and my projections for the future, on how I use a human-centric approach in how I lead myself, how I build teams, and how I build brands and businesses.

What I hope this book will achieve in doing is what I had wished for when I was a marketing manager aspiring to be a CMO—someone to teach me all this. This book provides simple, actionable tips for young and upcoming marketing managers on how to pursue their dream of becoming a successful CMO and purposeful leader.

That said, it is no magic, but a collation of all my personal views, thoughts and applications to personal leadership in becoming a purposeful marketing leader.

Conclusion: A Legacy of Knowledge and Growth

This book is not meant to be conclusive, but rather, a starting point for ongoing dialogue and development within the marketing community. It reflects my commitment to the principle of abundance and reciprocity: By sharing knowledge, we expand our collective capacity for innovation and impact.

I hope this book will inspire and equip future CMOs with the courage and skills needed to lead in the creation of brands that not only drive profit, but also make a profound impact on society.

By sharing these lessons from my journey and the insights gained from both successes and setbacks, I aim to contribute to the nurturing of future leaders who can continue to elevate the practice of marketing to new heights. Through this book, I seek to help others unleash their potential, guiding them on their path to becoming visionary leaders who can build and sustain brands with soul.

Perhaps this is part and parcel of me living my purpose and my way of giving back.

PART I

Personal Leadership

CHAPTER 1

My Origin Story

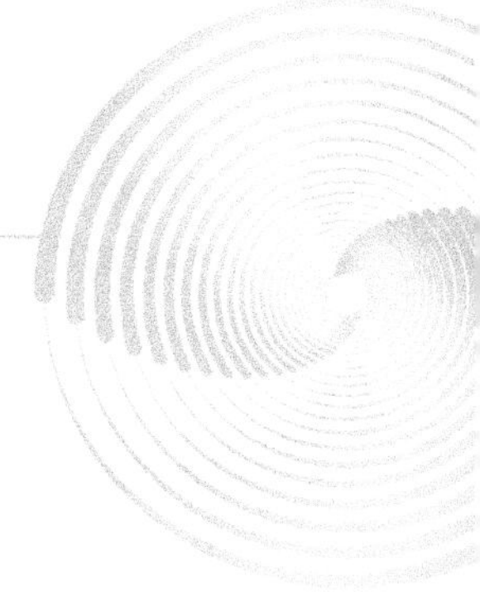

My story begins in the heart of Asia, in a humble Singaporean home. It reaches across the globe, into the boardrooms of some of the world's leading brands. It is not just a tale of my professional journey, but also of my lifelong quest to blend the science of marketing with the art of human connection. Born in Singapore, I am the middle child among three girls. My father, a retired journalist, and my mother, a nurse, greatly valued education. They instilled the principles of integrity, humility, respect and resilience in us from a very young age. My childhood home, though not affluent, was filled with discipline and love, setting a firm foundation for the life and career I would build.

I was six years old when the unexpected arrival of my youngest sister brought joy. But it also brought some complications. My mother struggled to manage her professional responsibilities alongside her additional maternal duties. This led to a decision that would have a profound impact on me—I was sent to live with my grandparents during the weekdays. Although this arrangement lasted for only a year, it shaped much of my early emotional landscape.

While living with my grandparents, I experienced a mix of nurture and a sense of abandonment. I was suddenly thrust into independence and self-reliance. While my grandparents provided a loving home, the distance from my mother during this formative time left me with a deep-seated need for her approval.

Despite these emotional challenges, I thrived academically. I attended Singapore's most elite schools, thanks to the sacrifices and foresight of my parents. My mother, ever the anchor of our family, ensured that my education was well-rounded and included the arts, music and sports, alongside academics. This holistic approach not only guided my intellectual growth, but planted the early seeds of my professional journey as well.

From primary school through university, leadership roles held a lot of allure for me. In primary school, I was the head prefect and in secondary school, I chaired the drama society. These roles were not just positions of authority, but opportunities to earn the recognition from my mother that I craved so deeply. They were my first forays into understanding group dynamics and the art of persuasion—skills that would become pivotal in my marketing career.

These early experiences made me professionally ambitious and competitive, but thwarted my emotional development. I became fiercely independent and competitive, and very guarded about my emotions. I was overly cautious about whom I could trust, on whom I could rely, and with whom I could be vulnerable, resulting in a very small inner circle.

The Journey to Becoming a Marketer

As I entered university, my career aspirations were still undefined. Growing up, my dream was to be an artist, a vision I'd nurtured since the age of five. Simultaneously, I was captivated by the prospect of becoming a doctor, fuelled by my love for science, chemistry and biology. Somehow these early interests foreshadowed the blend of art and science that would later underline my approach to marketing. I was naturally gifted with languages—I speak English, Mandarin, and I took on Japanese as a third language. This gift of languages certainly helped me understand multicultural nuances when I became a marketer.

During my second year at university, a fortuitous internship at Scott Paper (now part of Kimberly-Clark), was a career-defining breakthrough for me. That summer internship turned out to be an amazing experience, as the directors of the programme were ex-Unilever marketers and they curated an amazing brand-building and marketing programme for our small group of interns. That was where I first learnt that marketing is an art, as much as it is a science. It was fascinating for a young student like me, as it involved understanding people and delving into human behaviour. It introduced me to the complexities of consumer psychology, brand positioning, decision-making and the vital importance of cultural awareness—especially crucial in a diverse society like Singapore.

After graduation, I was determined to hone my skills at the mecca of marketing. I applied to two of the world's best schools of marketing, aka the world's leading companies renowned for their marketing prowess, Procter & Gamble (P&G) and Unilever. My efforts paid off when I was recruited as one of the top graduate trainees at Unilever. This set me off on a path that eventually led to me becoming the CMO at a multinational corporation.

Training at Unilever was tremendously educational. I learnt the essentials of classical brand building and started developing commercial acumen. More importantly, I fell in love with the craft of marketing and committed to it wholeheartedly. My passion for marketing stems from a fundamental interest in human psychology—understanding the human mind to build and position brands with a soul that resonates on a deep, emotional level.

My career-long marketing practice has been a continuous process of learning, observing and listening, skills that allowed me to uncover valuable insights to tailor the right value propositions for brands. I learnt how to harness both the science of data and methodologies, and the art of creative thinking. This fusion mirrors the integration of my academic interests, allowing me to effectively apply both my analytical and creative brains. Thus, my marketing career is not just a profession, but as well, a fulfilling adventure at the intersection of my lifelong interests.

* * *

After five years with Unilever, I had the wonderful opportunity of working at Mars, the world's largest privately owned packaged goods company. Despite its scale and size, Mars has been a family-owned business for over a century and it was my golden chance to work with and learn from the passionate entrepreneurs.

Then, the Asia-Pacific region was run by a third-generation owner of Mars. As a young and ambitious marketing manager, I was armed with all the marketing and sales training from one of the world's biggest Fast-moving Consumer Goods (FMCG) corporations. I jumped into a company that had far fewer processes in place, was highly entrepreneurial and was run on a handful of simple corporate values. It was an experience that you would either hate or love!

I am a very achievement-oriented person and I like to push myself to keep learning in new situations and challenges. I thrive in ambiguity and jobs with a large scope. In my second year at Mars, I was given an amazing opportunity by the regional president. He said to me, "I am giving you a blank piece of paper. Go and study the acquisitions we have bought in the sweets and confectionery category with the owners, and come back to me with a business plan on how to grow the sweets and confectionery category in Southeast Asia (SEA)." I was only 27 years old and it was a dream come true. I quickly packed my bags and flew to Australia and South Africa where both the acquisitions were located respectively, and spent weeks with the leaders of the companies. It was a fascinating opportunity where I sharpened my business acumen and intuition. I learnt how to run a profit and loss (P&L) statement, and how to craft "cash/profit" upfront. I learnt how to develop products and how to test, learn and experiment.

My entire career up until this point had been smooth sailing and packed with successes. I was brimming with excitement and overconfidence. One of my follow-up projects was launching Skittles Sour in Thailand. This project was a big step for me, as it followed my successful pitch of a three-year strategic plan to the company owners. We crafted a comprehensive launch strategy, which included advertising, road shows and merchandising, all coordinated through my team and the sales department.

The product recipes were not new, but they were packed in Indonesia and shipped to Thailand for sale. However, in the rush of these activities, I overlooked a crucial detail. I trusted the R&D director to handle product testing, a decision that soon proved costly. Just two weeks after the launch, we faced a serious issue: The candies began to melt due to Thailand's heat and humidity. It was a massive blow to me and my team. We had no choice but to recall the product, a decision that was both disappointing and humbling. We responded quickly by replacing the faulty products and fortunately, the retailers were satisfied with our swift action.

This experience was tough but valuable. It taught me a crucial lesson about the importance of thoroughness in every project phase. I learnt that it is essential to verify every detail myself, even if it means questioning the experts. The R&D manager, who was new and from Australia, was unfamiliar with Thailand's climate, which led to inadequate testing. This small oversight highlighted the need for me to be more proactive and involved in every project aspect, ensuring that all team members are fully prepared for local conditions. This incident was a turning point for me, teaching me to never assume that all bases are covered and to always double-check, especially when working in new and unfamiliar territories. Thankfully, our company leaders were supportive and did not penalise us.

Most importantly, as I worked closely with the Mars family, I picked up some more humanistic qualities from them. These are people with humility, who are willing to listen with empathy, especially when they talk to the consumers they are serving, the lady in the pantry or the worker at their factory line. They know them all by their first names and have no ego or airs about being the owners. They seem to have endless reserves of energy which they bring every day to their work. Each one of them is anchored to a strong personal purpose that guides them to the creation of their brands and the growth of their business.

As I got to know them and their purpose better, I learnt how learning, curiosity and a growth mindset are game-changing qualities in any profession. Their resilience to bounce back from failure stems from their attitude and openness. One of them gave me a book on meditation and asked me to start practising so that I could control my thoughts and better align my whole being. I didn't know it then, but perhaps this was the start of my journey to becoming an intentional, human-centric leader.

After my transformative five-year stint at Mars, I got another great opportunity in a leading luxury beverage company, Diageo, where I spent 10 years growing, learning, applying, falling, rising, firefighting and going from strength to strength. Two things were working in tandem for me: My insatiable appetite to learn and succeed, and my great fortune of working alongside some of the best mentors and sponsors in the industry. The first 20 years of my career would have felt surreal if I hadn't given it my blood, sweat and tears.

However, life is rarely a fairy tale for most of us.

Even as I basked in my professional glory, externally, I became a hard and emotionless individual who was battling constant self-doubt and fear internally. The big, bold strides I made at work and all the recognition that came with it, became my crutch. It was my way to get my mother's attention. I constantly wanted a newer and shinier trophy that I could use to prove my worth in her eyes. My relentless pursuit of my career goals was coming from a position of fear and self-doubt, rather than a place of abundance. I constantly sought external validation for my professional accomplishments instead of acknowledging my innate gifts and talents.

This love-hate relationship with my mother lasted a long time. I am sure this affected her too, as well as other members of my family. It finally ended eight years ago when she was on her deathbed. My mother had been battling stage-four pancreatic cancer and passed away within two short months of her diagnosis. In her final moments, she apologised for what happened when I was six years old. She acknowledged the significant impact it had on me and expressed her gratitude for the independent, courageous woman that I had become, an individual that so many people can rely on; for serving as the anchor for our family and caring for so many around me—except, all these years, I had forgotten to care for myself.

My mother's death marked the beginning of a different personal leadership journey for me.

I was finally ready to address my inner demons and make peace with myself. Without realising it, I had been carrying the trauma of rejection and abandonment my whole life. Being one of Diageo's top leaders, I was fortunate to have a coach who helped me on this journey of discovering my purpose and working on my personal development. Confronting this incident has helped me face my fears and my persistent self-doubt, and most importantly, accept myself for all my potential and my flaws, both professionally and personally. In the last eight years, I have embraced my whole story, in all its imperfection, and spoken openly about it as part of my leadership journey.

Two years before my mother passed away, I became a mother to a baby girl. I was determined not to become a shadow of my mother. I did not want to repeat the same approach with my daughter. I started working on my fears and self-doubt. I started letting go of my perfectionism, lest my daughter imbibes it from me. She continues to inspire me to be a more wholesome person, in complete alignment with my purpose. Instead of imposing rules on my daughter, I have tried to empower her to be herself and embrace the best version of herself. Instead of imposing my expectations on her, I help nurture her virtues while giving her the space and opportunity to make mistakes. She is a beautiful blend of both my husband and me, showcasing merits and traits from both of us.

The confluence of all these experiences has greatly affected my current professional image and leadership style. Professionally, my leadership style has become more authentic, vulnerable and inclusive, resulting in considerable progress as a growth-oriented leader who values human connection. The way I present myself externally now aligns more closely with my inner self. I want everyone to see the true essence of who I am, what my purpose is and how genuinely I care for all those around me. I am not afraid to be authentic and lead by example in living my values. My authenticity and inclusive leadership have resonated with several people at work and beyond. Over the past eight years, I have successfully built high-performing teams and driven cultural and organisational transformations. Many of my team members appreciate and connect with my inclusive and purpose-driven leadership style, gravitating towards my vision and approach.

My work with my inner self is far from over. Whenever I feel stressed or whenever the external environment does not feel fully aligned with me, I tend to relapse to the same patterns. During such times, I am unable to be the best version of myself and struggle to showcase my full potential. The most challenging aspect is the persistent voice in my mind that asserts, "I am not good enough."

In January 2024, I faced a significant and unexpected career challenge. Many of the events that unfolded seemed nonsensical at first and I felt like a major failure. However, I soon realised that this experience was meant to teach me a valuable lesson and was, in fact, a gift of abundance of time and energy to adjust my perspective once again. I started working with my coach to realise that because I hadn't accepted my six-year-old self, I had been settling and compromising on certain choices at work. I was always choosing to prioritise the needs and desires of others over allowing my own potential to fully blossom. Fatefully, as a strong believer in intention, my own purpose is centred around unleashing other people's potential to build impactful brands, businesses and teams.

This career hiccup was yet another wake-up call for me. I began reconnecting with my inner six-year-old, embracing her full potential and nourishing her soul with self-care, self-love and positivity. Through accepting and caring for myself, I started to hear my voice clearly and began radiating it with boldness and courage. I was already a magnet for talent and a voice for youth and female talent. By embracing this inner-girl and her potential, I started making radical shifts in my life, both personally and professionally.

I still consider myself a work-in-progress and a big part of this ongoing journey involves embracing my true self. I have learnt the importance of not compromising on my values, setting clear boundaries and filling my life with love, all of which has been incredibly liberating. This approach has not only brought me inner peace but also begun to attract positive changes, leading to new opportunities and opening doors in ways I hadn't anticipated.

If I were to condense all my life lessons into one fundamental insight, it would be that growth is inherently non-linear. It is essential to have the support of mentors, sponsors and coaches in both your career and personal life. These guides are invaluable as they help you realise your innate potential, reconnect with your soul and encourage you to evolve into a better version of yourself.

Through my 25 years of experience in marketing and with a keen sight set on the future, I have come to strongly believe that understanding the soul of human beings will differentiate great businesses and brands in today's world. Establishing emotional connections with yourself and others, deep curiosity, agility and a creative mindset are the keys to unlocking growth in the future world.

CHAPTER 2

How I Found My Purpose

I was a straight-As student and an accomplished student leader. The first 10 years of my career were smooth sailing. My deep-seated longing to achieve, underpinned by my keen aptitude, bolstered me to succeed and rapidly rise above the competition.

During the initial five years of my career at Unilever, I was trained at the best marketing "school". After the tenure, I had the amazing opportunity to work with entrepreneurs at Mars for five years, tackling various challenges that came with building up businesses from scratch at the young age of 27. This crucial period marked the awakening of my business intuition and nurtured an appetite for innovation, setting me on a path to sculpt thorough business models of my own. Life became tough yet exhilarating; I was always high on the adrenaline rush of non-stop wins and achievements.

It was during my time at my third company, Diageo, that I encountered some challenges that forced me to reorientate myself and how I had acknowledged my achievements so far. As the regional brand director at the time, I had to reinvent a second brand of whisky in the Asia-Pacific region. This involved leading a team of indirect, cross-functional members from around the world, none of whom reported directly to me. I poured my heart and soul into learning how to unite team members whose values were not necessarily alike, nor were they completely aligned with the brand vision. However, something felt amiss. The orthodox mantra of hard work and persistent planning just weren't sufficient to motivate them. I realised that it was not enough to just win over my team members. I also had to lead by example.

In those moments, I found myself constantly battling my inner demons—self-doubt and fear. After all, work had not only been a mere part of my life, but it had also consumed my entire identity. I was fortunate to be guided by a coach who created a safe space for me to find my own purpose or my ikigai, the Japanese term for "a reason to live", i.e., something or someone that gives you a sense of purpose for living.

Purpose gives meaning to your existence. It makes your life more wholesome. People often ask me why we need an ikigai. The answer may not be the same for everyone, but finding one's true purpose in life nurtures a sense of fulfilment, happiness and meaning. As a work-in-progress myself, I will always remember this.

How Do You Find Your True Purpose?

There are many books that talk about purpose, such as Simon Sinek's *Start with Why and Find Your Why*. I was inspired by *Ikigai: The Japanese Secret to a Long and Happy Life*, written by Hector Garcia and Francesc Miralles. The framework I borrowed from their book shifted something deep within me. It felt more than just a new concept. It was the push I needed to alter my perspective.

> *"We cannot control our emotions, but we can take charge of our actions every day. This is why we should have a clear sense of our purpose."*
> —Hector Garcia and Francesc Miralles

Framework for Ikigai

Your purpose lies at the intersection, or rather, the alignment of these four elements:

- Passion: What you love
- Profession: What you are good at
- Vocation: What you can be paid for
- Mission: What the world needs

Figuring these out is a far-reaching process and takes time. And if there's one fundamental truth my life experiences have taught me, it's that growth worth striving for is never linear.

The Journey of Finding My Purpose

I consider myself incredibly lucky to have spent the first 20 years of my career under the guidance of exceptional mentors who had complete faith in my potential. At Unilever, Mars and Diageo, they recognised my strengths and traits, and most importantly, they saw potential in me that was yet to be unleashed. It's truly a blessing to be at the receiving end of such opportunities and luck.

Finding my purpose has been a liberating experience, but it is also marked by doubts, fears and insecurities.

It was through coaching that I was able to trace my life's trajectory and early experiences. Being a middle child and living with my grandmother, away from home at the age of six, left its mark on my emotional narrative. The bright side of it is that it made me self-reliant, achievement-oriented and turned me into a natural leader. It also taught me to see opportunities in every problem I faced.

On the dark side, my motivation stemmed from a place of fear, abandonment and feeling neglected by my mother. I disliked that it was my deep-seated fear, rather than passion, that pushed me to become overly ambitious, self-confident, or in other words, a hard-nosed person. I was tirelessly competitive, forthcoming and not exactly someone who could win everyone's hearts.

Together with my coach, I realised it was time for me to face my inner fears and that meant talking to the six-year-old me. The sense of abandonment I felt as a child formed mental habits that I was not aware of. Later in life, these got in the way of discovering my passions, skills and my future self.

I had to peel back layers and layers of self-doubt to get to the root of my unfiltered identity. It was also during this journey that I discovered my true calling. I am passionate about the cultural, artistic and data-driven aspects of marketing, and I seek to have a deeper understanding of the human mind, to inspire a deep emotional connection between brands and the stories they share.

I am skilled at shaping brands and businesses that stand the test of time and positioning organisations that prioritise the needs of their customers, thereby creating value for shareholders. I wish to excel at what I do and become a global CMO.

It aligns with my mission of elevating brands and businesses to create more meaningful experiences for people, society and communities. Brands that are human-centric and authentic can have a much stronger impact, not only on profit, but also on humanity. This affirms my vocation of getting paid to perform the role of a CMO.

These core principles define me. They are my North Star. They are why I wake up every day, why I do what I do, and how I approach my personal and professional life. If it weren't for coaching, I wouldn't have been able to craft my purpose with such strong conviction.

I must also not forget how, through the process of finding my life's purpose, I had to confront my inner fears, especially the hidden aspects of myself which had not yet been revealed. This meant aligning the image I create for others externally with my inner self, the need to let go of my ego and establish a perfect balance between the heart, mind and soul.

To better position myself as a CMO who embodies her true purpose, embracing the empathetic and caring side of myself has never been more necessary. It became clear that I needed to develop leadership skills that also recognise my vulnerabilities and strengthen my resolve to walk the talk.

It was when I began approaching my leadership role from a more humanistic perspective that I began a new chapter in my life. Over the last eight years, this fostered a strong feeling of community and belonging, which led me on the path to becoming a human-centric growth leader.

ACTIONABLE TIPS

1. Do not shy away from confronting your inner fears. Self-awareness is the first step on the road to understanding yourself.
2. Allow the wisdom of ikigai to steer your thoughts and emotions.
3. Seek out a skilled coach to guide you through this life-changing process of self-discovery!

Why Is It Important to Discover Your Professional Purpose?

Over the last 25 years, my career has been a fulfilling adventure, thanks to all the amazing opportunities I encountered at some of the most iconic brands. This reinforced my belief in purposeful leadership, granting me the freedom to mould my own leadership framework from scratch. The first hundred days of every role I take up are dedicated to creating a vision. I invite all team members to come together and craft a common purpose that guides our marketing efforts.

I consider this to be a crucial step as deep down, each of us desires to belong to something greater than us, a vision that fuels a meaningful purpose. As marketers, we must pave the way for this transformation, building a common path towards growth.

Team's Strategic Vision

This framework makes it possible for me to shape my team's strategic vision. More importantly, it encourages personal buy-in and motivation.

The seeds of real change are sown through alignment towards a common vision which embodies the "what"; clarity in the strategic plan, which is the "how"; and a personal commitment to the underlying purpose, otherwise known as the "why". Such a process of co-creation is invaluable as the voice of each team member matters in this journey.

Leading with Heart and Authenticity (In Life and Work)

Before I present concrete examples of this framework, I must emphasise that personal leadership and understanding your inner self go hand-in-hand. Having spent the last 16 years in the alcohol and technology industries, both extremely fast-paced and competitive markets, it is easy to lose yourself in the constant race. I was fortunate enough to work with mentors who focused more on my strengths and helped me unleash them. It was with the help of these coaches that I gained more clarity and a better sense of direction in shaping my own purpose.

I used to think that building a leadership image was just about external appearances. However, as the years went by, I learnt that leading from a position of authenticity, being true to yourself and inspiring others to do the same has a much stronger impact. To be able to do that, you must first know your superpowers and strengths. Only then you can assert your voice.

"Leadership is about making others better as a result of your presence and making sure that impact lasts in your absence."
—Sheryl Sandberg (Former COO of Facebook)

The path to discovering my authentic self was not something that "just happened". It took a great deal of hard work, many sessions of coaching, and an innate desire and willingness to dive deep into my inner self. It demanded a lot of work, time and constant deliberation, but the results were truly rewarding.

For me, this journey began 16 years ago when I was working at Diageo. It was a time marked by some challenges that made me realise how unhappy I was. This was when an ex-colleague suggested that

I work with a coach. Though I was sceptical at first, I took a leap of faith and started working with H (abbreviated name), marking a new beginning in my life. Through our sessions, I was able to fully explore, for the first time ever, my strengths, beliefs and values. I was finally peeling back the layers of myself, which revealed a clearer picture of who I was and who I wanted to become.

Deep down, there was always a yearning for something beyond work, something more meaningful—an anchor that could ground me. Together with my coach, I realised the importance of introspection as a tool to not only hone my passions and professional skills, but to also reconnect with my soul. I moved closer and closer to crafting my own purpose, an anchor that has stayed with me these last 16 years. I continued to evolve this purpose as I progressed through the different phases of my life, both at home and at work. Having spent a good amount of time in this mindset, my approach to purposeful leadership changed drastically. As a marketer, the guiding principle that underlies my work is my resolve to create meaning for brands, teams and society. This fits perfectly into my mission of building brands and my passion for understanding the human mind. What keeps me going is the aim of making a lasting impact so others like me can continue pushing organisations forward.

I have achieved a more harmonious balance where my external projection as a leader reflects my inner self more authentically. Being aware of my own weaknesses, I choose to surround myself with people whose skills complement mine.

What Does Purposeful Leadership Look Like?

My belief in unified wisdom and perspectives, and my role as a marketing leader keep me true to these work ethics. These are responsibilities that I will never delegate:

- Establishing a clear vision and direction
- Aligning stakeholders and peers with the vision
- Allocation of resources to bring that vision to life
- Creating an environment that nurtures the best qualities in my team members, which holds them accountable with the help of measurable KPIs

Leading from the Heart

In the last 10 years, I have worked a great deal with Gen Z across the globe, especially in the Asia-Pacific region. This experience was both fascinating and eye-opening—fascinating because it made me realise how much I love being surrounded by the limitless enthusiasm that they have to offer and eye-opening because it showed me that they highly value brands driven by a meaningful purpose. Not only that, but Gen Z will take you seriously when you, as a leader, employer or company, also embody your intrinsic, deep-rooted purpose.

So, it is no wonder that a leader guided by these values gains a following. He or she is someone who genuinely cares about others' growth and unleashed potential.

Having said that, leading from the heart did not come to me naturally. It took years of working with them before I learnt to adapt my leadership style to include the following:

- **Be personal and authentic:** Speak from a place of authenticity and emotion, and don't be afraid to show your vulnerability.
- **Stay engaged:** Practise genuine care and be generous with your advice and mentorship. Listen with empathy.
- **Prioritise communication:** Send weekly emails to inspire, convey your vision and encourage productivity.

Bringing Back the Power of Storytelling in Leadership

We all love stories that give meaning to our reality and experiences. I never knew that storytelling mattered in leadership, but I do know that an important trait of a good leader is to have a strong presence and inspire a compelling vision.

My career so far has taught me that the essence of leadership lies in the stories we share. I would like to write about two such stories that embody this lesson.

First Story: Inspiring M.A.G.I.C. with the Asia-Pacific Team

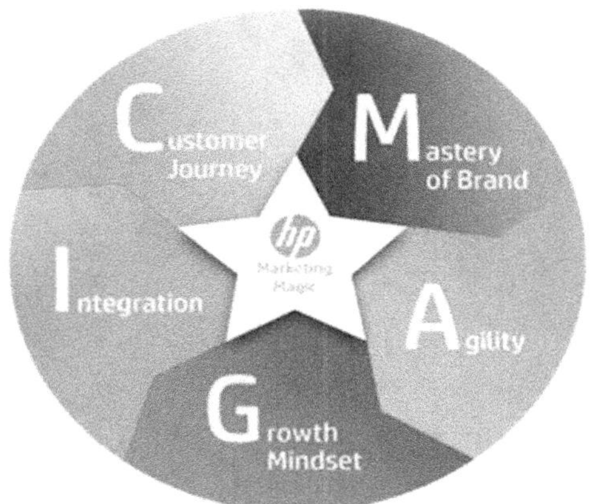

Inspiring M.A.G.I.C.

In 2021, after my success catering to the global market, I was beckoned back to the Asia-Pacific to take on a new, challenging role. As I seized this opportunity, it became clear to me that I had to focus on creating a brand new plan, which meant communicating with my team.

But nothing is ever as simple as that, is it?

I quickly learnt that in this new "normal" of constant change and uncertainty, striking a healthy balance between burnout and mental well-being is the need of the hour. This led me to create a North Star as an anchor for my team.

Within the initial two months, my team designed a binding manifesto. This manifesto was more than just a document. It highlighted key aspects of our purpose and what we want to stand for as an organisation. It also defined how we could use this North Star to unleash the potential of each and every member of the team across the Asia-Pacific.

We worked together to craft M.A.G.I.C. and its five guiding principles: **M**astery of brand, **A**gility, **G**rowth mindset, **I**ntegration with other functions and **C**ustomer journey. The manifesto represents every need of a marketing organisation, with customer insights as the starting point. Next is the mastery of building brands that stand the test of time, and finally, completing the transaction through integration with business partners to achieve profitable business outcomes.

Another force that drives the manifesto forward is a growth mindset. We are often told that change is the only constant and as a marketing professional, I couldn't agree more. Customer behaviour is volatile; business models are constantly disrupted by digital transformations; trust in brands is threatened by ESG needs around the world. For a leader with a growth mindset, this would mean staying humble, listening with empathy to customers, and finding valuable insights through data to constantly reinvent the business and the brand impact.

As for staying resilient in the face of change and challenges, agility is the antidote to complacency. It reminds us to put our egos aside and constantly learn, experiment and adapt from our successes and failures.

While these ideas might seem basic, even obvious, staying true and anchored to M.A.G.I.C. allows us to continue honing our craft to build influential brands and businesses.

The Second Story: Reignite Belief in the Global Insights Organisation

A year later, in December 2022, I was given the opportunity to lead the Global Insights Organisation, a group of talented experts from around the world. The brief was to reframe the organisation and harness the team's full potential to have a measurable impact on the business. In my first hundred days, I was fully dedicated to listening to the team's enthusiastic discussions, as well as several stakeholder interviews. I could sense an opportunity there to transform the organisation from being perceived as just an in-house research organisation to one that stands out as a strategic, trusted partner. There was also room for growth in relation to reshaping the team. This inspired me to cultivate a belief that they could evolve from good to great. To this end, we designed the manifesto below:

A GREAT TEAM: OUR MANIFESTO

Image courtesy of the Global Insights Organisation.

The purpose of this manifesto is very simple: It captures the team's collective belief in their unique strengths. It aims to unite the community as one and motivate every member to voice their own ideas.

These two examples are by no means perfect, but they are my personal experience of how I integrated storytelling into my approach to leadership.

S☉UL INFUSION TIPS

1. Discover your unique purpose. Once you realise what drives you, things will start to align naturally.

2. On the path to change, creating a brand narrative is necessary. Winning over both stakeholders and the teams you lead, either directly or indirectly, is more important than inventing a fancy marketing plan alone.

3. Incorporate the P.A.V.E. manifesto into your leadership style. An approach I have developed is:
   - **P**: Personal
   - **A**: Authentic
   - **V**: Vulnerable
   - **E**: Engaged

PART II

Business Leadership

CHAPTER 3

Building Brands with Soul

What Is the Heart of Marketing?

I love marketing and have spent 25 years as a marketer, but I am not here to bore you with the theories and framework of marketing. I'm sure there are already several books out there talking about that. What I do want to share is why I am so passionate about the craft of marketing. I want to ensure that I continue to hone this skill of mine and always up my game. More importantly, I believe in the law of reciprocity. Ergo, by sharing with others, my proficiency will enhance in return.

The first marketing book that was presented to me was *Positioning: The Battle of the Mind* by Jack Trout and Al Ries. It highlights how marketing means understanding human minds, their needs, wants and motivations. These needs and wants are then turned into products, services and solutions, packaged in a compelling way that makes consumers want to buy them. Sounds simple enough, right?

Of course, the role of a marketer has evolved tremendously and with the rapid advancement of technology, has become quite complex now. But even today, amid multiple meetings and reviews, and stakeholder management processes, there is one aspect of my job as a CMO that I consistently enjoy and would try to never delegate. It is finding that penetrating insight that answers a pressing business problem; a question that aims to solve a human need or at the organisational level, to steer the business to see its problems through a customer-first lens.

At the heart of marketing lies the diligence, curiosity and patience to discover a breakthrough customer insight. Now, is this all just art or is there some science to it? Some might say that marketing is solely an art. I beg to differ. Marketing is a fusion of art and science.

What do I mean by this?

You will need data to help you look at macro trends, the human needs and wants, and ultimately, analyse your business or brand situation. With the right data analysis, you can develop a great insight. Once you have your idea and value proposition, you will also need science to validate this proposal. I believe the artistic side of it lies in the creativity of developing solutions and bringing them to life in engaging ways and touching the hearts of customers. This requires curiosity, creativity and innovation. It needs an insatiable appetite to understand the different cultural nuances of different consumer generations, across multiple geographies and cultures.

The craft of marketing is the sum of art (creativity) and science (data). It utilises both the right and left hemispheres of the brain. Perhaps that is why I am so grateful that my mother empowered me with an upbringing that gifted me with development in both art and science, which made me ready for this amazing marketing work.

I do love art. I often personify the role of a marketeer akin to an artist, painter or sculptor. The brands and the businesses we have built were born out of our passion for creating a masterpiece.

I remember I was recently invited to speak at an event where I was asked how important the role of data in marketing is. My answer is: It ensures business alignment, translates activities into financial terms regarding margins and revenue, and substantiates our business cases. It is crucial in enabling us to help build an engagement plan throughout the customer's journey. We must have the ability to make sense of the data and keep asking "why, why, why" to draw out a piercing insight to build a marketing programme that will make people buy the business offerings or change a certain behaviour. That, ladies and gentlemen, is the art behind the science of the data.

Just as when Leonardo da Vinci was creating his masterpiece "The Last Supper", he must have calculated the number of variations of how he could draw the reverent scene. But it was his experience, mastery and interpretation of the emotions that helped breathe life into the soul of the masterpiece.

A Brand with Soul

Throughout my marketing career, I was blessed with the most amazing opportunities to work on many iconic global brands: Johnnie Walker, Hewlett-Packard (HP), Dove, Lux, Anlene, Wall's Ice Cream, M&M's, Mars, Pedigree, Skittles, Snickers, Vaseline, Smirnoff, Guinness, Baileys, Talisker and the list goes on. Each one of these brands has its own amazing story of heritage. They stand on the shoulders of giants. But most importantly, each one of them has a "soul". I use this word quite often and it is almost synonymous with part of my own brand. So, what is the "soul" of a brand and why is it so important?

Perhaps the most famous definition of it comes from the retired CEO of Starbucks, Howard Schultz. In his last note before his retirement, he mentioned that "soul", as described by the Webster dictionary, is:

- The moral and emotional nature of human beings
- The quality that arouses emotion and sentiment
- A spiritual or moral force

The soul of the brand is intangible, but it is so endearing when you know of it, when you see it, and when you feel and experience it. There is no guideline to follow in building a company or a brand with a soul. It is an amalgamation, a tapestry of several singular events, collected over many years in the reservoir of the company's core purpose and its *raison d'être*. It does not emerge from the company's strategy or tactical execution. It is born out of love, passion, and the responsibilities of its leaders to simply do the right things for the customers they serve, for the stakeholders, for the employees who wear the brand logo proudly every day, and for the community.

I love the phrase "the soul of the brand" and I've had many opportunities to reframe and reimagine both a global brand to local relevance and build up a local brand to global presence. I am beginning to apply this phrase that I use often with my stakeholders: To build a global brand with local soul or scale a local brand up to global scale. The phrase "global brand with local soul" is often present in my narrative. It is a critical part of my strategy and language.

Building the soul of a brand leans more towards the artistic side of the marketing craft.

Global Brand, Local Soul

I have helped many iconic brands align their global brand positioning to local relevance. This has become a trademark of my marketing mastery. I was thinking of how to explain a brand with soul with a more appropriate example that embodies the philosophy "global brand, local soul", but instead, I will use examples that are not brands I have led before.

The closest example I can think of is McDonald's. The company has a strong, consistent brand positioning, with a very clear brand logo (the golden arches), brand semiotics (Ronald McDonald) and signature products like the McCafe, the Happy Meal, the McSavers, etc. One thing that McDonald's does very well is in empowering their local team to adapt the company's global guidelines in a way that aligns with the local culture. This is represented in their go-to market strategy, their marketing and even their products. An example of their local menu is the Samurai burger in Japan. The way they market is reflected by their recent Korean boy band partnership. This showcases their empathy and appreciation for the culture, as well as the ability to build a global brand with local soul.

Another example, which is closer to home for me, is the "Singapore", aka the country.

Singapore is known for being efficient and safe. It is the hub for financial, aviation and regional headquarters for foreign MNCs and start-ups. You can see this from its constant presence in the top 10 best-global-cities-to-live-in index. However, the creative and technological sides of things are not well-positioned. With her quest to diversify her identity as more holistic, Singapore embarked on a repositioning exercise recently to attract more tourism and be associated with art and creativity. The country took a bold stance to expand the musical landscape and attract impactful foreign musicians and artists into the nation. It kicked off with the exclusive Taylor Swift Eras Tour concert that was only available in Singapore. Not only did this give the country a huge economic uplift, it also brought alive the intangibles of the Singapore brand. After the Taylor Swift concert, there was an influx of visiting international stars. The experiences, the vibes and the views towards Singapore evolved to one of energy, creativity and bustling with attraction. It is an experience that you can make tangible, even though it is an amalgamation of emotions, experiences and feelings.

This is an amazing example of a local brand built for local, but done in a way that has global scale. The impact of positioning Singapore as a destination for concerts and global artistes has already delivered benefits and impact. It gave the country massive publicity worldwide and repositioned Singapore beyond just a hub for finance and aviation.

Multi-stakeholder Impact

The work of building a brand is no longer one to serve just the consumers. It does not belong to just the marketing department anymore. In the last few years, with the transition of macro, societal and economic verticals, brands and companies need to stay relevant, not only to address their customers, but also to multi-stakeholders. They must satisfy their customers, employees, shareholders, influencers, government personnel and their partners. Most importantly, the message must be consistent and not transactional. It must be authentic and experiential to create (in a world of turbulence and pretenders) a sense of belonging with its people and a sense of humanity with its customers. It must stay true to its "centre" and its heritage, and yet, be relevant with the times (i.e., the macro trends). It must be nurtured, protected and preserved, yet compelling enough to propel the business forward.

Developing a brand with soul is both an art and a skill. I don't profess to be an expert in it, but I have had some significant hits with the great opportunities I was given. The work must be led by leadership with a sense of purpose and courage to drive change and impact. It must be given a direction that is courageous enough to bring alignment across multiple internal stakeholders and functions. It must be communicated in a heartfelt manner and be authentic enough to win the hearts and minds of the employees and convert them into brand ambassadors. You must apply the science of marketing with data to bring alive the soul of the brand, from the logo, the advertising and the experience, to the holistic sensorial journey of smell, touch and feelings.

Perhaps, this sums up my own lived experience of how to build a brand with soul. In the following chapter,

I will share a lot of examples using two use cases of how I built brands and inspired multi-stakeholder impact.

Most importantly, this brand stewardship requires both personal, purposeful leadership and a village of like-minded community leaders aligned to a common goal, in order to build a company or brand with a soul.

SOUL INFUSION TIPS

1. Marketing is a craft of both art and science.
2. You need to have a penetrating insight to build brands with soul.
3. A brand with soul needs to serve multi-stakeholders in order to create a legacy.

CHAPTER 4

Building Businesses with Soul

"There are those who look at things the way they are and say why. I dream of things that never were and say why not?"
—George Bernard Shaw

Purpose vs Profit

As I look past my professional pursuits, I have to say that I have been very fortunate to work for companies that are founded on the shoulders of iconic giants, fantastic culture and values. Most of them are also very purpose driven. As I reflect on these experiences with the different stints I had across Unilever, Mars, Diageo and HP, they all have one thing in common: A very well-articulated mission that is purpose driven to the impact the company wants to create for the multi-stakeholder they serve, so as to deliver shareholders value.

There have been lots of articles, literature and even debate around "purpose vs profit". Can a purposeful company deliver profit? I truly think that purpose and profit can coexist. It goes back to the clear articulation of why the company exists. It means clearly defining the stakeholders the company wants to serve and what is its unique reason for why the company exists, then authentically ensuring whatever they do end to end shows up to that purpose.

Perhaps the best in-class example of purpose statement will be that of "Patagonia":

Patagonia's Purpose Statement

"We're in business to save our home planet.

At Patagonia, we appreciate that all life on earth is under threat of extinction. We aim to use the resources we have—our business, our investments, our voice and our imaginations—to do something about it."

Profit and purpose go hand in hand. Purpose guides you to deliver your true unique competitive advantage of the business and helps one make money. You need profit so as to re-invest into the business and deliver good impact for the stakeholders.

Big Hairy Problem(s) to Solve

Let's face it. We live in an era of turbulent time. Post-pandemic, this world event has created huge disruption with the emergence of multiple macro trends and caused disruption to the world's supply chain, and how our future of work looks like. With societal unrest, climate changes and massive technological advancement in the Industrial 5.0 Age, the challenges faced by companies, CEOs and C-suite leaders have accelerated to huge daily challenges. The usual known business models are quickly replaced with new disruptive business models, often facilitated due to technological advancement. Some of these challenges are almost insurmountable.

I often pondered hard at what are the key problems businesses should exist to solve in this era of the future of work. To name a few:

- What are the opportunities and challenges of re-industrialisation in the US, Europe and Asia, including implications for capital, labour and community?
- What is the best view of the future and what are the implications for what we need to start doing today?
- How do we focus on moving the needle on sustainability despite funding and affordability challenges?
- How will the convergence of multiple exponential technologies change our business models?

- What are the new dynamics of supply chain resilience and the way in which companies and countries compete?
- How can we consistently deliver on our purpose and ethical practices across our organisation, beyond pure compliance?
- How do companies, corporations and the government deal with the rising issue of mental health?
- What characteristics should the next generation of leaders have and how should these be developed?

These are just a few big hairy problems that corporate leaders and CEOs are often bombarded with, but the list goes on.

In order for companies to decide how to solve these questions and choose what big hairy problem to solve, they need to start with their purpose: Why do they exist, what their customers want and which stakeholders they would like to impact. This is where the power of purpose comes in.

In recent years, "purpose thinking" has become one of the hottest thought leadership concepts, promoted at every marketing and management seminar. Today, it is at risk of being simply forgotten about or "postponed until after the recession", as you sometimes hear in boardrooms. The issue is that purpose is linked to just ESG topics, as opposed to the overall mission of the company and in fact, how it impacts profits and also helps create sustainable pricing power.

The Power of "And"

Warren Buffet's number one criterion for investing in companies is the company's pricing power. Pricing power is a powerful concept that is still not as well understood by marketers as it should be. As Buffet has defined for decades, pricing power is "the ability to systematically raise prices without curtailing demand or losing share to a competitor". Marketers need to start getting obsessed with the pricing power and how to help their companies create a "sustainable pricing power". This is where the importance of long-term brand building comes into play. This is also where marketers can earn a business seat and even increase their opportunity of getting into board roles.

Pricing is tangible. Pricing power is hard data that trumps the fuzzy return on investment (ROI) discussion and any other marketing metric to convey the impact of marketing. It is the language of money that the chief financial officer (CFO), CEO and board want to understand. Pricing drives the top line. Investing in brand health today means pricing power tomorrow.

The best marketing companies are the ones that never waver on brand building. I happen to work for a few of them. They invest consistently, both in good times and in recessionary times. The key benefit lies in boring consistency, not in flashy brand relaunches that make for good media stories (and make or break marketing careers). They systematically build sustainable pricing power over the years and they monetise this effort on a continuous basis. The recent inflation spike becomes a moment they have been diligently preparing for. Inflation is not a crisis. Inflation is an acid test for a company's true marketing capability excellence.

In his 1994 bestseller *Built to Last*, management guru Jim Collins introduced the concept of the "tyranny of the 'OR'", which "pushes people to believe that things must be either A or B, but not both". Instead of feeling oppressed by this, he argued that highly visionary companies liberate themselves with the "genius of the 'AND'", the ability to embrace extremes of dimensions at the same time.

There is another often overlooked "hidden turbo" side to pricing power that CMOs might want to make their CFOs and CEOs aware of. It is visualised in the simple yet powerful concept of the "value stick", created by Harvard professor Felix Oberholzer-Gee in his 2021 book *Better, Simpler Strategy*.

Creating the "willingness to pay" (WTP) is the top-line concept marketers rightfully (and uniquely) should continue to focus on. However, now look at the bottom of the value stick. Companies can also grow margin by lowering costs. Not just by smartly cutting costs in the classic sense, but by elegantly leveraging pricing power to further lower what Oberholzer-Gee calls the "willingness to sell" (WTS)—i.e., the lowest price a company can accept for a product or service.

Intuitively, one can see how a company with aspirational, strong brands—i.e., brands with sustainable pricing power—gains a number of hidden WTS benefits that can put a turbo on the full margin, including (but not limited to) the below:

- Employees: May join and stay longer at lower cost
- Debt: Banks may offer lower interest cost for lower risk
- Equity: Investors may pay more for your shares
- Suppliers: May accept better payment terms to get you as a client
- Customers: May accept you as a reference supplier at lower cost
- Regulators: May accept lower risk-mitigation cost

This clearly demonstrates the impact across its stakeholders. Both WTP and WTS help drive margins. This is where the power of long-term brand building comes into play. Building a brand with soul helps drive sustainable pricing power. It is all about "balanced growth". It is about purpose and pricing power (and hence profit).

Howard Schultz wrote in his #1 *New York Times* bestseller *Onward*, the story of how Starbucks fought for its life without losing its soul. Articulated in his conclusion is the notion of "balance growth" where he talked about the power of the "AND".

"If Starbucks is to be a company my father would have felt proud to work for, a company that my wife and children and our partners' families will hold in high regard, we have to maintain balance on many fronts. Balance between the emotional and disciplined. Between instinct and information. Between global and local. The personal and professional, and, of course, between profit and humanity. Doing so will not be easy as we expand our brand and businesses around the world. But the sheer power that Starbucks Coffee has to positively affect the lives of tens of millions of people—partners and their families, customers, farmers, shareholders—is as invigorating for me as opening my very first store."

Servant Leadership

Now, let me come to another observation I made after having worked for purposeful brands and corporations. This is about leadership type.

I chanced upon the book *Good to Great* by Jim Collins 15 years ago when I was still with Mars. In the book, it was mentioned that from a survey of companies that moved from good to great, these "great" companies that performed financially well and yet have impact for the wider stakeholders they served, are often led by leaders who embody "servant leadership".

When I read this, it was coincidental that I happened to be given an amazing opportunity to understudy the founder of the candy company Mars acquired in Australia. His name is Chris Hadzilias and he stayed on with the Mars Asia-Pacific region as a consultant to help us drive our sweets confectionery category then. I understudied him for three years.

It was through that experience that I really learnt and experienced what "servant leadership" is all about. On the surface, these servant leaders seem quiet, introverted and full of empathy, and these traits can be mistaken as weak, in contrary to the expectation of assertiveness and aggressive influence. These leaders embody the following powerful traits, if you look beyond the surface:

- "One that puts the company, business and people good ahead of himself."
- "Serve a larger purpose for the business he or she created."
- "Profound display of humility."
- "Empowering and bringing the best out of teams."
- "Not afraid to make tough decisions for the greater good."
- "Unwavering commitment to mission and longer good."
- "Build community."
- "Foster psychological safety."
- "Relentless protection of organisation's interests."
- "Genuine care for others."

Collins recognised that the great companies are often led by leaders who exhibit servant leadership traits. I believe that building business and brand with soul is not an easy feat. I also believe that servant leaders are the ones who do it well and especially during turbulent times. I gave the book to my then regional president who is the third generation of the Mars family and he in turn shared the book with his leadership team.

Don't get me wrong, I am not a CEO and have not founded or led a company before. However, I have worked for many leaders and CEOs, and I found that being able to build a business with soul, purpose and moral compass requires a stoic leader who is anchored in purpose himself and practises servant leadership.

Creating Belief Inside Out

Having a clearly defined purpose is just a start. Creating belief and conviction inside out is a critical enabler to building business with soul. Having the right culture is a critical enabler.

This is by no means conclusive, but it is a firm belief that I have. Creating the right purpose and having a clear strategy is the start. Having a clearly well-defined brand purpose is just a start. The ability to galvanise the entire organisation and employees, and to create a belief inside out will be a magical potion to drive flawless execution.

I learnt about this quickly in the organisations that I have worked in. I have also worked for multiple CEOs and CMOs who start with creating and igniting the belief "inside out". We often overlook the fact that the employees and partners are your number one customer, and they are your best brand ambassadors. I have, hence, begin all my assignments on repositioning or building brand by igniting the belief from inside out. I have also created frameworks on how to galvanise employees and stakeholders across all levels and functionality.

Building a business with soul is hard work and certainly not an easy feat or for the faint-hearted. It requires a clear purpose, a relentless pursuit of creating a sustainable pricing power through the balance of building the long and short of brand building and purposeful servant leadership. But the journey and result are extremely rewarding.

Next, we will cover some examples of how I build a brand with soul and the leadership learnings I have gained from doing so.

SOUL INFUSION TIPS

1. **Purpose and profit coexist:** Companies can successfully integrate a purpose-driven mission with profitability. A clear articulation of a company's purpose not only guides its operations but also enhances its competitive advantage.

2. **Big challenges for leaders:** Post-pandemic, companies face significant challenges, such as supply chain disruptions, sustainability issues and evolving business models due to technological advancements. Leaders are urged to identify and address these "big hairy

problems" by aligning their strategies with their company's core purpose.

3. **Importance of pricing power and the power of brand building:** The concept of pricing power is highlighted as crucial for business success. Companies that can raise prices without losing demand demonstrate strong marketing capabilities. Long-term brand building is essential for sustaining pricing power, which ultimately drives profitability.

4. **Purpose-driven companies are often led by servant leaders:** These servant leaders come with differentiating traits and qualities that make them successful.

5. **Building business and brand with soul is best done by igniting belief "inside out" with the employees in the company:** It works better when your own employees have the same belief and become your best brand ambassadors.

CHAPTER 5

Keep Walking: Growing a Global Brand Locally

A Case Study of Johnnie Walker China

I would like to share an experience on an amazing brand growth story that I had when I was working at Diageo. I was leading the transformation of Johnnie Walker in China at that time. This is the story of how I built a global brand with local soul. In 2010, I was seconded into China with a couple of my peers. China is the most important growth market in the world. It impacts Diageo's performance on the stock exchange and the company's investors seek expansion in this market. We were the second-best player in the market, shortly after Chivas Regal, from the house of Pernod Ricard. In Asia-Pacific, except for China and Japan, Diageo was leading in first place. The company decided to send a few high-potential and high-performing executives to China to embark on an ambitious three-year plan of transformation and growth.

Although we were the second-best player in the field, as a brand, while we had strong awareness and equity, we were seen as an "old man's brand". The Gen Z focus group told us, "This is what my dad will be drinking." The Chinese economy was booming and new social media trends were emerging, e.g., the Sina Weibo. It is a generation of the 1990s and young Gen Z who seek progressive experiences and involvement, and participation in conversations. They are proud of the nation's progress and want to contribute to the progress stories. At the same time, the '70s to '90s generation is blessed with highly disposable income and the luxury market is just burgeoning with many foreign iconic luxury brands entering the Chinese markets, opening store after store. It was a time of rapid growth, filled with vibrant opportunities.

I led a group of like-minded individuals across agencies, both internal and within our distribution partner, and worked on a plan to make the iconic Johnnie Walker brand relevant to the Chinese culture with an intent to drive double-digit growth in three years.

That was the business problem statement.

The consumer problem statement was to make an iconic brand relevant to Gen Z and transform the perception towards a premium and luxury brand. This would in turn drive profitable growth. We started with a customer-first mindset and looked at the '70s to '90s generation's perception of the Johnnie Walker brand, their interpretation of progress and their expectation for the category. Through deep understanding and data analysis, we found the following two inter-generational cultural insights:

- They want to participate in the conversation on their nation's progress.
- They want to be seen as "in the know", especially when it comes to exclusive knowledge, e.g., knowledge of whisky and culture.

Two initiatives were born out of these two insights and we developed the following triple bubble:

China Johnnie Walker

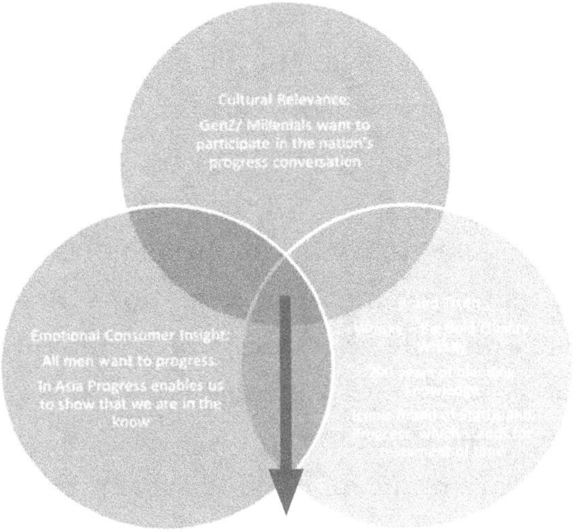

Johnnie Walker Inspires Personal Progress

With these insights in mind, we came up with two disruptive initiatives that were industry-first and category-first. Yes, we were intentional in being disruptive in approach. As a challenger brand, we needed to stand out from the clutter.

Initiative One: Opening of Johnnie Walker House

Gen Z and young millennials do drink a lot of whisky. In bars and nightclubs, they drink whisky cocktails with mixers and sometimes even with green tea. However, nobody appreciated the heritage of the whisky nor understood the power of the story behind the whisky that has been aged for more than a decade (at least).

I recall my experience when I first joined Diageo. In my first month of induction, I was sent to the distilleries in Scotland to learn all I need to know about whisky. I remember sitting at the round table with one of the most knowledgeable master blenders. He not only started teaching me how whisky is made, but also the craft of blending behind the whisky product. The conversation lasted for almost three hours and it was one of the most fascinating conversations that included both the art and the science of whisky making.

This experience left a huge impression on me. When we were brainstorming ideas to make the experience premium and to educate the younger Chinese generations about whisky and its culture,

I thought: What if I bring this experience of whisky culture to China?

Scotland whisky conversation.

Limited edition whisky that marries Chinese culture with the Johnnie Walker brand.

We borrowed from other categories like Nike store and other iconic luxury brand retail stores. These retail stores were sprouting non-stop in China. This gave me an idea—what if I were to bring the intimate whisky conversations I had with the master blender to China, in an intimate exclusive space? I was sure that many Chinese people who want to show off their knowledge would love to be a part of this experience. We worked with a London-based boutique agency to create the first-in-the-world exclusive, luxurious, and intimate Johnnie Walker House (the first in the world luxury experience centre) from scratch and sold this idea to stakeholders. Surprisingly, it was endorsed at the headquarters and within a short three months, we managed to launch the world's first Johnnie Walker experience centre. This was initially a branding idea, but it also got monetised with the sale of high-end limited editions, and even customised casks. Within a year, we brought thousands of high net worth Chinese through the Johnnie Walker House doors. This idea generated a lot of buzz in the Chinese market and globally. Most importantly, it started premium-ising the brand. Of course, we complemented this with other super-premium portfolio strategies in other parts of the Chinese market and channels.

Initiative Two: Recruitment of Generation Z Campaign

To make an old man's brand relevant to the young progressive Chinese, I believed that we needed to tell real progress stories in an authentic way. The Chinese seek and look up to local influencers. Hence, we decided to work with world-renowned Chinese documentary filmmaker Jia Zhang Ke. We started telling three-minute long, real and authentic progress stories of the 12 most famous influencers in China. The way it was launched was also disruptive as we engaged in a "progress" debate on the leading social platform Weibo.

The campaign generated an engagement of 90 million people in a short one-week span and became the talk of the town very quickly. It also started the first documentary, a three-minute short film format (the Chinese call it *weidianying*) and became a "Keep Walking" platform for the next three years. As a result of this campaign, Johnnie Walker became relevant to the Chinese young generation.

These two initiatives were highly successful and set ground-breaking norms for the category and industry.

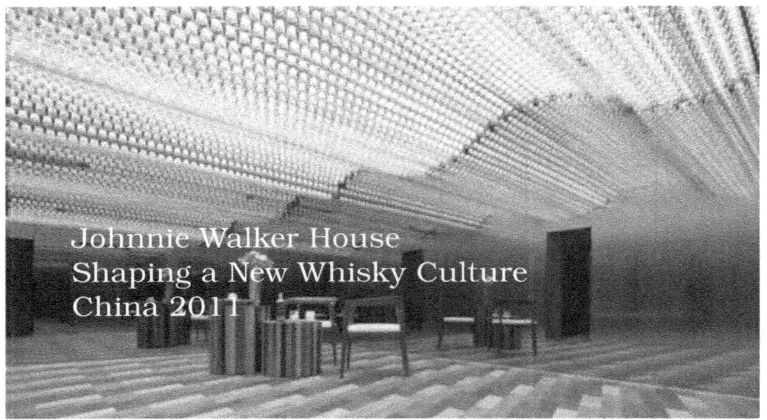

First Johnnie Walker House in Shanghai and globally.

Combining Emotion and Data: Leveraging the Art and Science of Marketing

There was a lot of data behind the Johnnie Walker and Gen Z initiatives. Of course, we had to make multiple business and 4Ps plans (product, price, place, promotion). We also developed brand strategies to sell internally with our local, Asia-Pacific and global leadership. These plans were backed by multiple sources of data with a financially sound business strategy. Then, to uncover the cultural nuances and insights, we generated a few hypotheses through a combination of data mining the social listening space, deep in-home visits and focus groups with leading influencers. Then, we applied creativity (the art of marketing) to uncover those piercing insights, and test our ideas and hypotheses. We also looked at associated categories and industries (e.g., luxury goods and sports retail) to learn from them and challenge our own thinking, assumptions and category conventions. We kept asking "why, why, why" until we got to the penetrating insight.

Behind those ideas were culturally relevant insights at a macro level, marrying the culture behind the brand, and bringing it alive in a bold and courageous way.

Bold and Courageous Leadership to Achieve a "Rocketship" Goal

This perspective goes back to the root of building brands, i.e., to go back to find a penetrating macro-societal insight and to seek disruptive and innovative ideas that can be borrowed from other categories. However, what is more transformational is leading and binding a group of cross functional teams across multiple geographies and agencies to come together and achieve a "rocketship" ambitious goal.

It is a matter of being bold and courageous and leading a community of people to win together. Until now, this campaign of making Johnnie Walker relevant to Chinese culture is a much talked about experience within the industry, as well as among partners and friends who have worked on these initiatives.

S☺UL INFUSION TIPS

1. Finding relevant macro and societal insights that can transform the brand narrative is important.
2. Stay true to universal global brand positioning, but find local cultural relevance.
3. Backup the plan with data (the "what"). The "how" is the application of creativity, human-centric insights and deep understanding of cultural insights to develop the plan.
4. Be bold, courageous and lead a village of collaborators to win and transform together.

CHAPTER 6

Game On: How One Market Can Power-Up a Global Organisation

The Story of Omen by HP Gaming Brand Becoming a Top Korean Player in 18 Months

I believe that a powerful brand with soul can help mobilise an entire organisation towards a common goal. In my 25 years of building multiple iconic brands, I have witnessed several such examples, one of which is fairly recent and quite a memorable success.

Business Challenge

Korea is the world's third largest PC gaming market with a huge growth potential. HP Omen Gaming was at the ninth position in Korea's e-sports category. It had low brand awareness, low market share and we had to find a way to stand out in this cluttered market.

In 2021, the global team, given the market potential, decided to invest in Omen Gaming. The marketing team that I was leading at that time, decided to come together to lead from the front to co-create the business and 4Ps plan with the managing director and the business teams.

When we came together to brainstorm ideas and build the plan, we aligned and agreed that given Omen's low brand awareness, it was important that we start with the ambition to build a brand with soul and "go big" on finding a socio-cultural tension that we can disrupt and own.

Now, this is where the magic of the marketing department comes in. We started conducting consumer deep-dive sessions with Korean gamers. Through multiple immersive forums, we realised that there was a macro-social tension that we could challenge and disrupt. Seventy-four per cent of the youth in their 20s believed that the Korean society experiences injustice or unfairness and that the "Korean society betrays hard work". Your success is determined by the class in which you were born and the silver spoon that you were born with. We decided to demonstrate that in gaming, especially the world facilitated by Omen PC gaming, there is no unfair privilege, only hard work that gets rewarded. We wanted to start with a strong stance against unfair societal advantages due to income or family background.

We kick-started a launch campaign called "We Don't Care" to say "Omen does not care about who your daddy is". We only care about your skills and hard work. Omen is here to enable the gaming community with its PC hardware, solutions and ecosystem for gamers to be their best and progress with us.

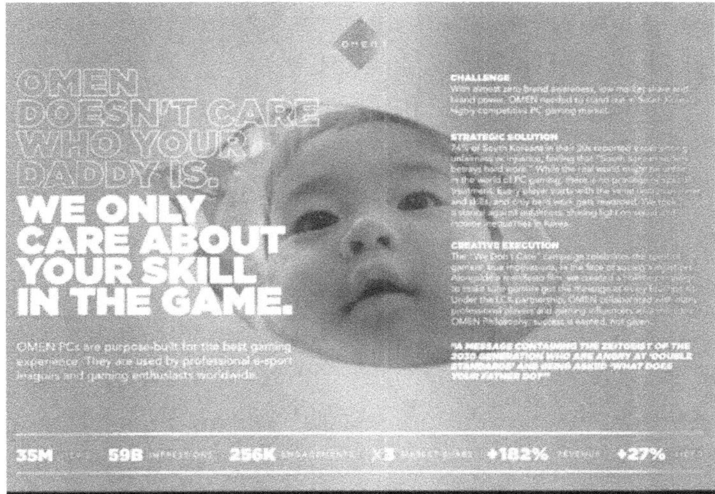

Executive summary of Omen's Korea campaign.

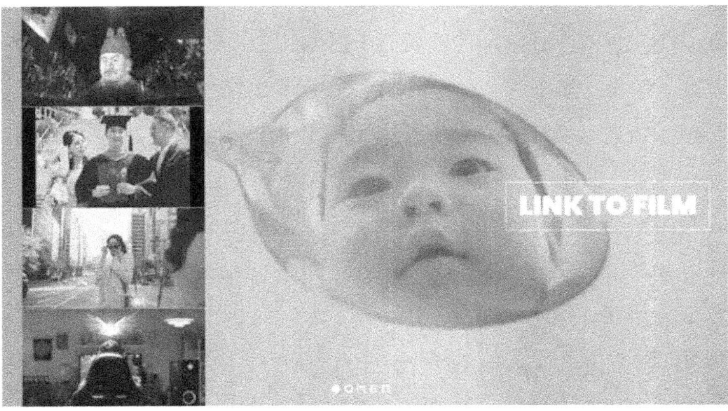

Extracts of parts of the first advertising campaign "We Don't Care".

The campaign insights and execution kick-started the journey of the pursuit of a brand with soul. The marketing team led from the front, not only in the launch of this campaign, but also worked with the business team to create a detailed 4Ps plan. We orchestrated each execution of events and experiences. The positioning of this campaign was able to strike a chord with gamers within the company and with our partners, and we started using them to be our catalyst of brand believers to sell the message and ignite belief.

A Brand with Soul Can Power-Up an Organisation and Create Magic

As mentioned earlier, when we decided to take this bold stance, the marketing team came together to lead from the front and power-up the organisation so as to make this investment successful. It was not within our responsibilities to develop a 4Ps plan, neither was it our job to convince the category leaders to think outside the box and be bold with their assumptions. Yet, we went on an intentional "stakeholder" influencing path. I had different people on my team "marked" to different stakeholders to create the right buy in. We were also intentional in needing to win the hearts and minds of the Korean employees, the sales team and the channel partners. This was in pursuit of making them our brand ambassadors or brand advocates.

On top of that, we were also clear in wanting to convert our key stakeholder, the managing director, to sign up to this work. He was sceptical at first, as this message is quite a bold stance to take in the conservative Korean society, but we sold with conviction and made him a spokesperson of this work and plan. We tied that back to the reputation he could achieve as we grew collectively to the number one position in two years. We never turned back—we started attracting influencers and key players in the gaming community, e.g., T1 and Faker (the number one Korean esports team) to work with us. The esports tournaments and the sponsorships of T1 and Faker were the gateway to rally the employees and channel partners. We were recruiting all of them to join us at the esports tournament to witness the power of Omen Solutions supporting the best esports teams to win the competition. The entire Korean market and the employees wore Omen Gaming t-shirts to participate in key esports leagues. You could feel the soul of the brand live in the spirit of the employees, the community and the partners we worked with. The rest is history.

We eventually became the top dog in just 18 months, ahead of our own initial internal timeline target of three years. This was a feat never done before in the Asia-Pacific.

The journey of building a global brand with soul shows that a label needs to have multi-stakeholder impact—across employees, partners, influencers and government officials. Marketers sometimes need to demonstrate leadership and to not be afraid to lead from the front, even if it means developing a full 4Ps business plan which is not your responsibility, as in this example. Establishing a global brand requires an enormous amount of empathy and curiosity for understanding the cultural context of the society and the lives of the target audience. We found a fantastic, sweet spot here and when a culturally relevant insight arises that resolves the target audience's tension, it creates movement. It shows how a powerful brand with soul can help power up an entire organisation!

SOUL INFUSION TIPS

1. A brand with soul has the power and ability to mobilise an entire organisation towards the same aligned goal and drive business growth.

2. Marketers should use such opportunities to develop a 4Ps plan to create multi-stakeholder impact.

3. Do not be afraid to expand your leadership to take on things beyond your own function. Marketers need to know how to lead from the front, drive collaboration and foster cohesion towards the same goal.

PART III

Friday Emails to *My Marketing Team*

"It has long since come to my attention that people of accomplishment rarely sat back and let things happen to them. They went out and happened to things."
—Leonardo Da Vinci

The da Vinci CMO Attitudes and Experiences.
(Credit: Institute for Real Growth)

With the advancement of technology over the last few years, the craft of marketing and the role of a CMO has become complex and fragmented. The average tenure for CMOs is around 43 months, with a burgeoning classification of titles ranging from chief growth officer to chief brand officer, etc.

I had the opportunity to be exposed to the IRG training. The institute, together with consulting firm Spencer Stuart, conducted multiple global surveys and demystified the role of the CMO. They summed up these experiences and attitudes under the umbrella term "da Vinci CMO".

I love art and Leonardo da Vinci is one of my favourite artists. I find the label of the da Vinci CMO extremely apt and fascinating. It elevates the marketing profession as a craft and captures the art and science behind it. Most importantly, it brings alive the importance of the humanistic aspect of marketing.

The picture above encapsulates the experiences and skills that a modern CMO needs to be equipped with. Where I like to draw attention to is the attitudes of a da Vinci CMO, namely, "Curious and Agile Learner", "Servant Leadership", "Connected and Collaborative", "Courageous and Inspiring Storyteller" and "Speed and Impact Obsessed".

Friday Emails

The next part of the book talks about my practical application of how I improve these skills, my inspiring rally cry and its examples to my team. Every Friday, over the course of the last six years, I spent some time reflecting on my ideas and learnings, and later share them with my team via emails.

This habit of Friday reflections started shortly after the Covid-19 pandemic. I lead large teams which are all scattered across the globe in different time zones. I feel that besides the team meetings, work meetings and some one-on-one with direct reports, some of the messages that I want to send to the team get reinterpreted and there is always a distance between me and the most junior marketers. It still lacks an avenue to understand, authentically, who I am as a leader, what is keeping me awake and most importantly, it reinforces the key "change or transformation" message. I like to demystify this aloof, far away approach of a leader.

I was inspired by both Howard Schultz (ex-CEO and chair of Starbucks) and Angela Ahrendts (ex-CEO of Burberry). Emails became a way through which they communicated their ethos, personalised who they are, and shared success and recognition. This was the start of these Friday emails or reflections, as I call them.

Without fail, in my recent role in HP, I painstakingly write weekly emails, regardless of how busy I am in the week. I always add some form of employee recognition. In addition, I talk about a certain leadership trait and experience that I want to reinforce with the team and share my knowledge with them. I find these Friday emails to be vital in sharing and reinforcing key change or transformational messages.

The response from the team has been overwhelming. It personalises who I am as a leader; it makes me more approachable; it also keeps communication and issues faced by the business timely, with speed and impact. It also demonstrates to the team that their leader does care deeply about them and will help them unleash their potential. It became a unifying platform that drives the consistently strategic pillars of the transformation vision that I had for the team. It becomes an easy jump-off point for topics when I get into group meetings or one-on-one conversations with the team. Some of them even commented that these Friday emails are what they look forward to as they start to wind down for the weekend.

I cover numerous topics with these emails, but the ones that resonate the most revolve around exactly what a good CMO needs to have and what a high-performing marketing team needs, to be ready to face the "unthinkable" world in which we now live. I cover topics such as, purposeful leadership, power of creativity, lessons learnt from AI, growth mindset, resilience and the leadership battle scars or experiences that I got while practising my craft as a da Vinci CMO. These emails recognise the team or team members who demonstrate one of the key attributes that is part of the transformation journey. These do not always come with a definite answer or solution. They just capture some of my own personal reading, experiences and my point of view on issues.

I chose to keep the tone of these emails authentic, vulnerable and personal as I want them to be a true reflection of who I am as a leader and the values of my brand. (I certainly do not use AI on any one of them!)

In fact, these Friday emails or reflections encouraged me to write this book. The more I share with the team, the more I learn about myself and, therefore, improve myself. It certainly hones my skill both as a leader and a CMO, and my passion for writing. I kept all these emails and I do revisit them every now and then to add more colour to the topics as I learn and grow through external experiences or from the team.

Some people keep journals to capture their gratitude and thoughts. Some artists have their sketches in their art books. So perhaps to me, these emails reflect the marketing craft, but more importantly, the leadership traits that define me and the lessons I want to share with my team and the world. I believe in the law of reciprocity. I certainly feel that the more I share, the more I learn, and the more I get back.

This part of the book captures a few of the many Friday emails I have shared with my team—across the self, the team and peer leadership.

I hope you like them. Friday reflections start here.

CHAPTER 7

Human-Centric Application in the AI Era

AI is just an enabler; it is all about the fusion of AI and Human Intelligence (HI) and Human Ingenuity!

Dear Team,

For the past few months, every other day we wake up to a new story on the latest AI innovation and all the things that the big tech firms are doing with AI. LinkedIn is swarming with everyone—from amateurs to professionals—sharing their "expertise" or their points of view on AI. It is almost overwhelming and to some extent, stifling even. In the boardroom, we have been asked many times about this, driven by the fear of missing out (FOMO) mentality, what we are doing to utilise AI to foster higher efficiency and productivity.

So, I thought I would dedicate this week's email to talk about generative AI and my thoughts on how it can help our marketing craft. I will share my point of view and try to bust some myths.

This evolution of AI is analogous to the invention of the calculator many decades ago or the Internet in the '90s. When a new generation of technological evolution begins, it comes with a certain level of fear and scepticism. For example, when the calculator was becoming mainstream, there were groups of mathematicians rioting against it. When the Internet came to be in the '90s, several people wondered what to do with it and whether it was here to stay. It decidedly was.

I believe that generative AI is also here to stay. The concept of AI has been around for a while now and it is going to stick. In fact, I believe there is more to come.

The right approach is to not fear it, to not fight it. We should embrace it and apply human ingenuity to it. I believe magic happens when "human intelligence" and "artificial intelligence" combine. AI will help us work faster with data, but it is the human mind that will draw the insights, the creativity and the values of what we want the product, brand and campaign to stand for.

We should not resist AI. In fact, we should get comfortable with this discomfort and really utilise the data generated from these tools to become more productive and better in our marketing craft. We must get comfortable with data analytics and the scientific side of marketing.

Now, I want to bust a few key myths.

1. You can turn over all your marketing work to AI

We should avoid relying solely on AI algorithms and instead only use these as tools to enhance our strategies. Human expertise and intuition play a crucial role in crafting successful marketing campaigns.

2. AI will take over all our work

AI excels in automating repetitive tasks with remarkable efficiency, enabling us marketers to streamline mundane work and focus on the more strategic and creative aspects of our jobs.

3. AI can perform just as well without human input

The synergy of human skills, such as creativity, empathy and understanding of human tensions, with AI's analytical capabilities, leads to the most impactful marketing outcomes.

4. AI is too complicated for you to use

We should not be intimidated by AI. It is accessible to all and meant to complement our efforts, not replace us entirely. By embracing AI, marketers can enhance their craft, automate mundane tasks and devote more time to generate piercing human insights and ideating innovative solutions that serve customer needs. The key is to approach AI with curiosity, creativity and fortitude to experiment. The collaboration between humans and AI can revolutionise the marketing landscape, delivering exceptional results.

So, what should we do to embrace AI to become more productive and effective, and help with our marketing craft?

First, I don't profess to know everything—I am learning these things at the same time as you. I think this is where we can all apply ourselves and put on our thinking hats to be a "curious and agile learner". We should adopt the mindset of learning fast, learning big and scaling up quickly.

1. Let's start small, think big, but act with agility

Let's start small with generative AI. You can experiment with ChatGPT and use it to help write an email or a newsletter and even brainstorm ideas. It does not need to be a big project. Once you get used to the tool, start playing around with different large language models (LLMs) so that you can reassign the mundane work. Divert this energy and focus on the strategic idea behind the work—the penetrating insights.

I recently tried using ChatGPT and DALL·E to help me create a presentation for a speaking opportunity. I had so much fun creating multiple versions! In fact, now I use AI to analyse several documents to create a one-page summary to share my learnings with the team at a much faster speed.

2. Let's lead by example

The AI applications teach me a lot about leadership. Clearly, to approach the best practices for generative AI use, it is not enough to lead just by telling people what to do. You need to lead by doing. Let the technology wow you, learn from it and use it to explore the right side of your brain.

I try out a new AI tool every day and attend one webinar a week so I can enhance my knowledge.

As I experiment more, my mind opens up to numerous possibilities and stimulates my creativity. I realise that I am more present to new thinking and new ideas. Hence, it helps with solving strategic problems in our daily work as marketers.

3. Let's learn through sharing

I have also started a bi-weekly meeting called *AI Learning Hour*. My intention for these sessions is for us all to share the learnings as a community. We learn faster when everyone shares their knowledge with others. Let's use this AI learning hour to create use cases for the best practices that can "lift and shift" to other parts of our work collectively.

4. We can apply and experiment with AI in several areas of the marketing value chain

We are starting to employ AI in the following areas for experimentation. In fact, AI can help us create better and more effective personalised digital journeys with a stronger impact.

- We begin by using AI in content production which reduces the turnaround time (TAT).
- We shift away from fixed segmentation to real-time behavioural segmentation with the help of AI.
- Some companies are experimenting with AI in product development by involving their communities in the concept creation of an innovation funnel. Some are also creating multiple versions of brand campaigns or experiences so that it gives the team a shot at a faster TAT.

However, ingenuity still lies with the humans who make the final judgement on whether to adopt this work.

5. Let's learn fast, learn big and scale up quickly

Unlike older business transformations, there is no fixed playbook to implement AI. You need to use human ingenuity to access AI's true potential. The core target is to learn fast, learn big and then scale quickly. It is almost similar to how well a LLM can predict, depending on the questions being used. These questions and framing these problem statements are birthed from the human mind.

It is all about the mindset

A recent Harvard Business Review article titled *Your Teams Should Drive AI Adoption, Not Senior Leadership* by Sowmyanarayan Sampath, the executive vice president and CEO of the Verizon Consumer Group, reinforces the above points.

AI is best learnt at the front lines. It is the people who do the work who need to experiment with these new tools. The learning should be democratised and employed to create a feedback loop for use cases. We should not be afraid to share our learnings and how we drive change and adoption. The world of marketing and building brands has rapidly transformed to adopt democratisation. We need to be adept at adapting. One of the more recent successful use cases was the organisation-wide adoption of AI in Moderna. They dedicated the creation and adoption of LLMs into teams of collaborators for individual functions. The teams used the LLMs to optimise their workflows. This accelerated adoption and execution of AI broke down the silos that generally exist in large companies. The productivity results were phenomenal.

How can AI help marketing leaders drive organisational transformation by creating a culture of learning and agility?

We live in a world where change is constant and transformation is the name of the game. We should apply the power of AI to reframe and democratise "learning and agility" to the users—the marketing team. I have seen the rewards of AI myself. If applied well, it can help marketing leaders drive and create a culture of learning. It can break down silos and enable teams to work in collaboration. Now, as a team, we are on a journey of transforming how insights can play the same role as a strategic trusted partner. How great would it be if we could evolve our research methodologies with AI and develop insights at the tip of the finger with a 24-hour TAT for our business stakeholders?

An iconic global brand with soul that adopted AI well is Coca-Cola. They were brave enough to democratise their creation of a global campaign into the hands of the creator community and some of their global advertising campaigns were co-developed with AI. Still, they did not forgo their basic principles of core brand value, key brand semiotics and visual identity principles.

The marriage of AI with human expertise in the marketing realm presents a powerful combination that can drive unprecedented success. The fear of AI replacing jobs is vastly overshadowed by the potential for transformation and the emergence of new opportunities. We must embrace AI as a tool to streamline the mundane tasks and focus on creativity and strategic decision-making. The key to harnessing AI's potential lies in approaching it with curiosity, courage and a willingness to experiment. By leveraging the unique strengths of both humans and AI, the marketing landscape can be revolutionised, delivering exceptional outcomes and customer experiences.

Dr Ayesha Khanna, a renowned Singapore-based expert in AI and founder of Addo AI, once said, "AI is here to maximise human potential."

I hope you learn from this experience and continue to be a curious and agile learner, and use AI as a partner.

Remember that you are the marketer; AI is just your partner and the future is in your hands!

Have a wonderful week!

Cheers,
Siew Ting

SOUL INFUSION TIPS

1. As marketers, we need to always stay curious and be an agile learner as the landscape changes so quickly. You must apply human ingenuity to AI.
2. AI is best learnt through experimentation at the front line.
3. AI can help drive transformation by creating a culture of learning and agility.

CHAPTER 8

Servant Leadership: Getting the Right People on the Bus

Dear Team,

Thank you for an amazing week and handling all the work in my absence. As many of you know, I just returned from the Aspen Institute. This is an annual leadership meeting where we take time off to really connect with our inner self and use it to sharpen our skills in "servant leadership".

After returning from a week of self-reflection, I would like to dedicate this week's email to the concept of servant leadership and how to build high performing teams:

1. Getting the right people on the bus

People often ask me, "Siew Ting, you have an amazing ability to identify people with potential and you know how to use this potential in roles that match them. How do you do this?"

Well, there are four questions that I always explore during interviews or in coaching sessions. They are as follows:

* What unique gifts do people receive from you, from being around you?
* What do you value?
* What do you stand for?
* What do you really want to create and find joyful to create?

Everyone comes with strengths (I call them "superpowers"), talents and underlying potential. They need to get the right role which will help them nurture this potential. Often, when I get into a new assignment, I first assemble a team of diverse people with diverse skill sets and talents that compliment mine. I seek out people with the right curiosity, growth mindset and a positive attitude towards growth, change and work. I will also ensure that there is room for these people to grow so that they are motivated to achieve excellence and do more. In the process, they build up their achievements.

Diversity is key to achieving excellence. I am a firm believer of diversity of thoughts and collective wisdom, especially in solving today's complex problems. My role is akin to "getting the right people on the bus". I want to create an environment of inclusion to inspire creativity and to solve the complex problems that we face daily. I call this a collision of the power of collective genius.

2. Creating a culture of inclusion and organic growth

A getaway to connect with oneself is critical in this turbulent world. I had the opportunity to introspect on my leadership style and what I would like to contribute to the world, and to each and every one of you.

I believe in the importance of creating a culture of diversity and inclusion. There is a lot of talk of inclusion at work, but different people have different interpretations of it. So, what do I mean by it? For me, this means that everyone has the confidence to bring their authentic self to work, regardless of culture, experience, gender or race. When they can be authentic, we can bring out their true potential and achieve impactful outcomes. To do this, we need to understand each and everyone's "superpowers" and enable everyone to assert them within the team so that there can be an interchange of ideas. I also see my job as one that provides you with the space and the tools (and training) with our partners to upskill you to be your best. We will dive deeper into this topic as we embark on modules on high performance soon.

Again, I don't know everything and I will be quick to admit it with radical candour, e.g., with AI. But I like to think that I can help frame the problem statement well, create the right environment to get to the solutions and align the resources to achieve the desired outcome.

3. Leading with confidence and empathy

Many of you lead teams. I want to share my perspective here on what the new world of leadership is all about. I have been observing people, especially Gen Z and millennials, for the last three years. Post-COVID, and in this world of constant reset and re-engagement, the future of work is drastically and rapidly evolving. Engagement levels are at their lowest and burnout is at its highest. As leaders, we need to navigate with confidence, but still demonstrate empathy. I'd like to clarify that empathy is not just about listening and consequently, lowering our standards. It is important that we maintain high standards and hold the teams accountable to their business outcomes. However, in the journey, we need to listen to feedback and the barriers faced by members to coach them to change their mindset and ignite their potential.

4. Creating a culture of trust will lead to high performance

We apply the trust barometer to building brands with soul, aka trusted brands. I suppose you can say trust is an equally important ingredient for a high performing team. Have you heard of the Trust Equation by Charles Green? In his work, he mentioned that trustworthiness is derived from how credible your words are, how reliable your actions are, followed by how intimate people feel towards you. As a leader, have you created an environment in which people feel mentally safe to speak up? Underpinning this is the necessity for a leader to have low self-orientation, i.e., it is less about the leader's own motivations and more about the team's requirements. That's what the leader should care about, along with the greater good of the whole team.

$$\text{TRUST} = \frac{\text{CREDIBILITY} + \text{RELIABILITY} + \text{INTIMACY}}{\text{SELF-ORIENTATION}}$$

Credibility (Words) – I can trust what he says about…

Reliability (Actions) – I can trust her to…

Intimacy (Emotions) – I feel comfortable discussing this…

Self-orientation (Motives) – Who does the advisor care about?

The Trust Equation.

All of you are leaders and you play a key role, together with me, in creating a trusted environment where everyone feels safe to bring their authentic self to work.

I care a lot about unleashing each and everyone's potential and together, we are the collective genius. For us to create a culture of trust, we also need to approach things with radical candour. As leaders, we should not be afraid to call people out if something is wrong. Likewise, team members should be able to return the favour and give you feedback when things are not right.

I guess the best example I can give is from a few months ago, when one of the junior-most team members called me out in a meeting where we had an external speaker. As an advocate for climate action and sustainability, she was disappointed with some of the actions of the company that the speaker represented. She also spoke without fear and questioned me for not having done enough homework in inviting that speaker. Now, I could have reacted negatively to this feedback, but I paused and reframed it as a good thing. In fact, it made me realise that this young lady was passionate, righteous and had grit. She has latent potential and if we put her in areas that she is extremely passionate about, she would thrive. Now, this is an example whereby I had to reframe the situation. It was less about my own ego and more about the team, environment and the culture we wish to create.

The Power of Community

Community. I love this word and what it represents.

You have probably heard me use it many times. I like this word because it has the concept of shared values. Wikipedia defines "community" as "a social unit (a group of living things) with a shared socially significant characteristic, such as place, set of norms, culture, religion, values, customs or identity". I think the modern world requires teams to operate as a community that has shared values, beliefs and in some cases shared goals and vision. But in these communities, there is no hierarchy and silos do not exist. It is about learning together, winning together and achieving together. Noticeably, using the word "community" symbolises an operating model that helps achieve the right outcome and high performance.

Leading teams in this turbulent world is both an art and a science. I compare this to the process of building brands with soul. It needs to start with empathy and here, the role of servant leadership encompasses four critical pillars:

1. Getting the right people on the bus
2. Creating the inclusive environment to unlock potential
3. Leading with confidence and empathy
4. Creating a trusted environment

Cheers,
Siew Ting

SOUL INFUSION TIPS

To become a good servant leader, you need to do five things:

- Get the right people—as diverse as possible—on the bus.
- Create an inclusive environment to allow people to be their best.
- Lead with confidence and empathy.
- Create a culture of trust.
- Leverage the power of community.

CHAPTER 9

It is All About the Business Impact

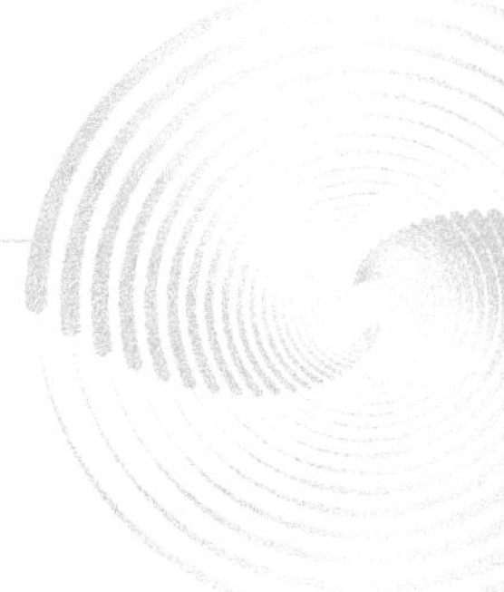

"Life is 10 per cent what happens to you and 90 per cent how you react to it."
—Charles R. Swindall

Dear Team,

I hope everyone had a good week!

I wanted to share a recent experience that I had while participating in a fireside chat. I was attending a digital day for a marketing event and the topic of this fireside chat was the ever-evolving role of a CMO. One of the questions that I was asked was how important is data in this new world of all things digital? How should CMOs embrace their role? What should they focus on, what is truly important?

I immediately reframed the question differently: What is the priority of a CMO in today's world?

1. It is all about business impact

Whether you are a brand manager, a campaign manager, a media specialist or an insights manager, it is all about creating a business impact! To put it a bit more simply, it is about creating growth for both the top and bottom lines of the profit and loss statement or creating value for the intangible assets in the balance sheet (e.g., increasing the brand valuation). It is too easy for marketers to jump onto the next big shiny thing. It is sexier and easier to launch the next Super Bowl ad or a new TikTok campaign. But at the end of the day, we are all doing these to deliver business impact.

Building a brand with soul or a business with purpose is no different. It is all about value creation and fostering growth. A recent S&P 500 report showed that shareholders in the top 500 MNCs are increasingly evaluating companies based on more than just tangible assets. The "brand" is a long-term intangible asset, so building a brand with soul becomes critical and quite relevant!

To build a brand with soul, marketers need to get back to the basics, i.e., the creation of an insight-driven 4Ps plan. Don't get me wrong. The digital journey and the audience mapping are important steps as well, however, they are but a part of the creation of this solid 4Ps plan.

2. Forget ROI: It is all about creating sustainable pricing power

Last year, I had the amazing opportunity to attend one of Chris Burggraeve's sessions, where he talked about purpose and pricing power as part of the IRG CMO gathering. Burggraeve is the former global CMO of AB InBev and former group marketing director of Coca-Cola, as well as the author of two books. He shared his proven concept of how purpose, if done right, together with long-term brand building, has the immense potential to impact pricing power. This, furthermore, has a direct correlation to profit and the creation of stakeholder value. We marketers get very excited with multiple "vanity" marketing input metrics, e.g., the click-through rate (CTR), impressions, etc., but we forget that these sound like voodoo to CFOs and CEOs. Pricing is tangible and we can demonstrate that we can create sustainable pricing power through our work in brand building—it is so tangible that it creates credibility in marketing function value. Hence, you must quantify value, not in terms of the ROI efficiency, but in terms of effectiveness—how can we create sustainable pricing power in building a brand with soul for the "intangible asset" of brand value.

Pricing power is a powerful concept that is still not understood by marketers as well as it should be. The incomparable Warren Buffet has defined it for decades now. In his words, pricing power is "the ability to systematically raise prices without curtailing demand or losing share to a competitor". It is his number one criterion when investing in companies.

As I said, pricing is tangible. Pricing power is hard data that trumps the fuzzy ROI discussions and any other metrics in conveying the impact of marketing. It is the language of money that the CFO, the CEO and the board wants to hear. Pricing drives the top line. Investing in brand health today means pricing power tomorrow.

In this article written by Burggraeve in *Marketing Week*, entitled "Purpose vs Pricing Power", he talks about the importance of a marketer truly owning and leading from the front in the organisation in terms of creating sustainable pricing power. The article also talks about how marketeers need to be seen as "levers of growth" and what it takes to become such a marketing enterprise. Purpose is part and parcel of creating pricing power and should not be considered separately. In fact, marketers need to lead from the front to create a brand purpose that impacts multi-stakeholders and, hence, stands for value creation.

3. Think enterprise-wide strategy, end-to-end and be the voice of customer

I know we don't own all the 4Ps in our company, unlike in the consumer packaged goods (CPG) industries where I spent my first 20 years. 4Ps is the basic marketing mix: Product, price, promotion, place. In fact, the 4Ps in this company are managed via three different functions. However, as we own insight and represent the customer voice, we are in a fantastic position to bring all the silos down and lead from the front. We do this by anchoring externally, starting with the voice of the customer. The more we think about an enterprise-wide strategy and end-to-end process, the more we are in a position to influence different decisions and demonstrate the value of marketing.

I have spent the last few years across the Asia-Pacific and globally, reframing the role of marketing beyond just the "colouring department" and towards building businesses with purpose and brands with soul by demonstrating their short- and long-term impacts. These are my six key learnings:

1. Extend brand building beyond marketing to a multi-stakeholder view across employees, corporate reputation, finance, shareholders and cross-functional teams within the organisation.

2. Quantify marketing ROI, but not just in terms of the short-term impact on efficiency. Demonstrate marketing effectiveness by talking about the value creation of intangible brand assets on the P&L.

3. Prove economic modelling on how the brand can impact pricing power. Be savvy with the language of finance.

4. Collaborate and connect with internal and external stakeholders to change the narrative.
5. Position the marketing function purposefully to employ it as a lever of growth.
6. Create distinctive brands with soul. In fact, drive business acceleration, i.e., adoption of new business models and recruitment of new generations of customers; with financial returns like revenue, margin or cash flow.

Effective brand management needs the power of "and"

Building a brand with soul has proven that the strongest brands have always been and always will be the ones that create sustainable pricing power. In marketing, we don't like the tyranny of the "or". Effective brand management is such an external high-wire act between the extremes—building long-term brand assets as cost-effectively as possible and intelligently monetising that asset value in the short-term. This contributes to the willingness to pay and the willingness to sell. Both of these drive margins. Developing the willingness to pay is the top line concept that marketers should rightfully continue to focus on. However, the lower the willingness to sell, the more the companies can grow their margin.

Now, this is where it gets interesting.

Positioning of building brand equity is linked to sustainable pricing power. This strategy delivers a number of benefits that can turbo charge the margin across its multiple stakeholders. For example, employees may stay longer at lower cost, suppliers may accept better payment terms, regulators may accept lower risk mitigation costs, banks may offer lower interest rates for lower risk (debt). So, speaking in the CFO language and tangible-ising building brands with soul in financial terms will be critical for a CMO or any marketer's success.

Whether you are building a purpose campaign, a performance-driven growth marketing plan or a digital campaign, ultimately, it needs to lead to business growth spoken in the language of finance, not marketing terms!

What are your thoughts on this topic?

Cheers,
Siew Ting

SOUL INFUSION TIPS

1. A marketer's number one priority is to drive business impact.
2. Forget ROI. It is about improving the pricing power.
3. Building a brand with soul or a business with purpose can help drive acceleration and become a "multiplier" of financial return.
4. The number one ally for any CMO is the CFO. Speak the language of finance.

CHAPTER 10

The Power of Customer Voice in Building Business Growth

Dear Team,

This week, I would like to talk about the importance of the customer voice in building business growth. Many of you who know me well know that I am passionate about the role of the customer voice!

At the recent Cannes Lion Festival, I heard a quote which resonated so much with me that it kept me reflecting about it for a while.

"The distance between the C-suite leader and the customers is perhaps the best metric of your company's brand health."
—Kory Marchisotto, Global CMO of
E.L.F. Beauty

This quote sent me down my memory lane. It reminded me a lot of my first 10 years in marketing and especially with my second company, which is an entrepreneurial company where I studied different entrepreneurs. I remember because the founders founded the company—we have an amazing, ingrained customer-centric culture—we are always making market visits and there is almost no distance between us and the customers. Visits by the CEO starts with market visits, followed by reviews and action plans on how to tackle these opportunities and challenges in the boardroom. Everyone from the CEO to the brand manager and the sales team always have the pulse of the customers at their fingertips. It was also through this experience that I learnt how to operate between strategy and action seamlessly.

Marchisotto shared in the presentation how she championed the customer voice and led from the front. Her best story was when she brought the CEO into a TikTok live and let him listen to the customers' feedback and within two weeks, a bronzer based on customer feedback was launched! She also spoke about how she mobilised every function of the organisation to participate in the live TikTok interaction with the young GenZ, including the legal department! She spoke with passion that every week she would look through the social listening tools herself to dig for insights instead of relying on her insights team, as she wants to lead by example.

I started reflecting on how real this is, as I got into the later part of my career. Did we let the bureaucracy and internal ways of working take over the core of the business we should be doing?

I am a firm believer of customer voice and I am an even bigger believer of how the customer voice will impact business strategy. As many of you know that in marketing, we are in the business of creating value. We are in the driving seat of understanding the customer needs and then marrying that with the company needs to create value. The intersection of customer needs and the company needs is what I will call the "Value Creation Zone".

In all my key CMO roles, I always had a head of insights lead as my right-hand person to help me co-create the marketing vision and strategy. However, as we get into trying to manage internal ways of operating, and the many meetings and presentations, we seem to stop listening to the customers' voices and start relying on research presentations or insights teams to tell and interpret the insights instead of having ourselves define the insights and being close to the customers.

Here are a few reflections and lessons for us to really think about this Friday afternoon. They are as follows:

1. Importance of customer voice in influencing multi-stakeholder enterprise-wide strategy: Perhaps keep it close, not through reports, but through mechanism close to the customer

I used to work for the third generation of a very well-known founder-led global MNC which is privately owned. He once said to me, "A great C-suite leader operates at the top and at the shopfront—the middle can be trusted and delegated to others." This really resonated with me.

As leaders, we spend a lot of time developing multi-stakeholders' enterprise-wide strategy and evaluation of performance towards the strategic plan. However, have we asked ourselves how often do we put the customer voice at the heart of the enterprise-wide strategy?

The other issue is when we get up the rank often, we start to rely on reports or what the insights team will do to interpret the information to insights, as compared to listening to the customers and finding the "truths" and "insights" for the brand and business we represent. In fact, with the rise of technology and AI, we can now hear the customer voice on an "always on" mode with social media available at our fingertips. I think we should improve our speed of impact by starting to measure ourselves with the speed of insight to action.

2. CMOs championing the customer voice will make them more successful

I belong to the camp of optimists when people talk about the CMO role being in crisis. Yes, no doubt, it has become more challenging, but I am a firm believer that the CMO is in the best position to champion the customer voice. The customer voice will be the most impartial view with an outside-in approach to really influence corporate strategies and identify macro growth opportunities. The customer voice can also help across the entire value chain, from product development, pricing, promotion to go-to-market (GTM). In fact, the CMO is in the best position to utilise the insights represented by the customer voice to influence and integrate the 4Ps together to create value for the corporation.

Perhaps this will help make CMOs more successful, more grounded, make them more strategic and successful, and be perceived to have the "T-shaped" skills to secure future board roles?

3. The insights function and leaders need to feel prouder of their expertise and perhaps lead the evolution of the function

I had the unorthodox opportunity to lead a global insights function. It was potentially the most unplanned career move as I am neither a researcher by profession, nor am I an insights professional. However, as I embarked on the transformational journey of reframing the insights function to strategic impact, I started to realise that the insights professionals need to indeed feel prouder of their expertise and what their craft can help with the marketing function to drive more superior and faster growth.

Call me an optimist, but with AI coming onboard and research can be done almost with immediate TAT, insights function needs to redefine their purpose more as the strategic trusted partner to deliver business growth with the discovery of penetrating insights. It is less about the research methodologies, but more about the outcome and the insights you will develop that will impact business decisions, outcomes and growth.

I feel that this is the time that the insights function needs to feel prouder of their profession and lead the charge with the CMO to redefine and let the customer voice be heard at the heart of the enterprise strategy. No one is in the best position than them to lead the charge to reframe the insights function with the power of their storytelling and data analytics skill sets to "illuminate" the insights for each business and human problem.

4. The insights function can be the "illuminator" of the business problem to be solved

I find that a lot of insights teams define their role as the market researchers, the data analysts and not the "illuminator" of the "why" behind the data. They often get stuck with the research methodology or are contented to be at the backroom presenting the market research presentation from the agency. I think the time is now for them to reframe their role and thinking. Nobody else is in the best position to shift their role to be the strategic trusted advisor and partner to the CMO and the business team to help solve the business problem. With the availability of multiple data, their deep problem-solving skills and their ability to integrate that to the human tension we are trying to solve for, they are best poised to reframe their role to be the "illuminator" of the business problem to be solved. I think the insights team should start being extremely close to the business, focusing on their storytelling skills to answer the "why" behind the data, being extremely comfortable with managing stakeholders, and being the champion of the customer voice in a more extroverted way.

I hope this email will start the movement of CMOs leading the charge of influencing enterprise-wide strategy by utilising the voice of customers and the insights function feeling proud of their profession to lead from the front with the CMO to drive the transformation of the insights function in the era of AI.

Anyone keen to join this movement?

Cheers,
Siew Ting

SOUL INFUSION TIPS

1. Influence enterprise-wide strategy with the power of the customer voice.

2. CMOs should start measuring themselves and their speed of impact with the speed of insight into action.

3. CMOs should work with their insights function to reframe the insights' role to be the "illuminator" of the business problem to be solved.

4. The insights function should be proud of their craft and with the emergence of AI, lead from the front to partner with the CMOs to be the customer's voice.

CHAPTER 11

The Importance of Creativity

"You can't use up creativity. The more you use, the more you have."
—Maya Angelou

Dear Team,

Last week, I was invited to Spikes Asia, and just like all events conducted by Cannes Lion, "Creativity Leading to Effectiveness" was the main topic. This was similar to the discussion held at the 2023 global Cannes Lion Festival.

It was interesting to note that while Asia has the highest adoption rate of AI in marketing (71 per cent in Asia vs 60 per cent globally), the freedom and empowerment of Asia marketers using creativity in their work is lower in percentage as compared to the rest of the world. In fact, many marketers are not making any headway in securing funds in brand building, as they have not made a "business case for creativity" at the C-suite or boardroom level.

This makes me think.

I am a firm believer in the need for marketers to exercise both creativity and data in their craft. Earlier, I spoke about the art and science of marketing. I also believe that creativity is no longer just what you do in campaigns or in creating great advertising. Creativity is a discipline that can be promoted and applied to problem-solving, developing new business models, innovation and leadership. The power that elevates this is the ability to link the creative impact with the financial modelling of business impact—in an econometric way.

We are increasingly moving towards a data-rich world where everything can be represented with big data and used by powerful algorithms that can sort and create patterns. In other words, when it comes to analytical tasks, we are no match for computers. Creative tasks, however, are a completely different matter. For me, creativity is all about the deliberate practice of achieving excellence in any field by continuously examining the situation through a fresh perspective and bending the rules to achieve something new. I believe, if creativity (backed with data) is practised not only in advertising and content, but also in all aspects of our marketing craft (business problem-solving, developing a new product, finding a new business model or even a new way of selling or going to market), it can be revolutionary and powerful.

But how can one truly embrace creativity in their work and bring this brilliance to help the craft of marketing and even leadership?

1. The pursuit of the aha! moment

I spoke quite a fair bit about the penetrating insight. I believe that the pursuit of the aha! moment within insight generation can also be applied to the pursuit of creativity. You must keep asking yourself, "Why? Why? Why…?" It is probably after five "whys" that you develop an enlightened idea or insight. This requires you to stay open to asking questions and reflecting on the answers until you have a breakthrough.

To achieve this, you also need to be exposed to the external macro environment, coupled with your internal experiences and knowledge to develop the right aha! moment and ensuing insights. In the creative process of a great campaign or an appealing advertisement, we call it the "one sentence brief" which captures the motivating insight.

2. Connecting the dots

Once you have the aha! moment, you need to start using the data you have to connect the dots to devise a solution. This process is almost akin to the incubation period in a startup's journey or a new product launch. You will connect the information to create a pattern and solve the puzzle to come up with the solution. This also requires that you leverage all the resources accessible to you.

3. The recipe for creativity: Failure and daydreaming
The recipe for creativity is failure and the ability to bounce back from this failure. You must see the process of failure as a way to create and find better solutions. What's even better is that you can use your "holistic mind" and combine the ability to dream to iterate on your ideas. A great example of this is the production or the creative review process in advertising. This is where you master and fine-tune new ways of storytelling.

One could argue that this just requires the brain's right hemisphere to dream. I disagree. I believe this requires one to tap into the subconscious mind as well. A very common hack for high-performing scientists and problem-solvers is to try thinking on the problem from various angles just before they sleep and let their subconscious mind work on the solution. Or even better, they meditate or do yoga before they go to sleep. They often wake up with different ideas for a possible solution.

So, are there any use cases of how I have seen creativity being applied beyond the traditional storytelling of advertising? I would like to share two instances:

Case Study 1: Leadership

Context

During COVID, my teams across the Asia-Pacific were stuck in situations where they no longer felt inspired and everything seemed to be falling into "business as usual" (BAU). Ideas were no longer flourishing and teams were not engaged.

Solution

Create a powerful "learning think tank" every Friday. During these sessions, teams come together to not only learn a new topic in marketing, but also collectively generate new ideas to drive business impact.

Results

Ten big and bold ideas were developed in three months because of this Friday think tank. This delivered three times the return on ad spent.

Case Study 2: Innovation

Context

Four years ago, before the pandemic, Asia's small- and medium-sized businesses (SMB) were growing tremendously and were an untapped growth opportunity. There were a huge number of startups and small SMBs that sought growth opportunities. However, what they needed was technological help and support, with China in the lead. The e-commerce channel was also burgeoning, with China leading the way on selling business-to-business (B2B) brands beyond consumer labels.

Insight

The Chinese SMB entrepreneurs sought a brand that can be a business partner to them, enabling and supporting their "fighting" journey throughout their entrepreneurship.

Solution

We developed a specific brand with solutions named, "ZHAN" (which means "fight" in Chinese). Not only did we create and enable technology that was more accessible to them, we also created an ecosystem that empowered the entrepreneurs to come together. This is highly differentiated as it is a business-model solution, compared to many other players who are out there delivering hardware. The business model was launched together with marketing engagement that tells the story of this startup and SMB's real challenges, turbulence and constant fighting journey.

Results

We built the number one leading SMB brand in China with the first-in-market direct-to-commerce brand. This model was then replicated in the rest of the Asia-Pacific.

The above examples are just a few use cases that I have experienced with my team, whereby we transformed creativity into business impact, which reaped great returns.

Therefore, creativity, if executed well, can certainly drive effectiveness and business impact!

Standing on the Shoulder of Giants

We talk a lot about building a brand with soul and a business with purpose. Sir John Hegarty, founder of BBH advertising firm, once said that many iconic global brands were founded on the shoulders of giants who are creators. They were not born CEOs; they were born artists. Walt Disney was an animator. Henry Ford was a mechanic. Coco Chanel was a fashion designer. Steve Jobs was an artistic engineer, but they all applied their creative experience in life, design and calligraphy to the creation of their first product.

Building Brands with Soul Requires Creative Genius

Building brands with soul requires strokes of creative genius and a spirit of courage to challenge the status quo. I want to talk a bit about one of the most iconic brands that I have worked for: Johnnie Walker. It is a 200-year-old brand founded in 1820. The brand truly stands on the shoulders of giants. It is beloved by whisky lovers, artists, creatives and it is certainly an icon of global culture. If you trace back its heritage and history, you will find that it is nothing short of multiple strokes of creativity. From the moment Johnnie Walker was founded in 1820 in a grocery shop in Kilmarnock, Scotland, it has been a treasure trove of creativity. Johnnie Walker whisky is sold in square bottles as the founder then started exporting globally and a square bottle is the most space conducive.

Secondly, the label on the bottle is slanted at a 24-degree angle. Why? So that it provides the most space to vividly present the label of the whisky.

In 1908, the iconic striding man was created by cartoonist Tom Browne. He drew it on a napkin while having coffee with the founder and it was then adopted alongside the global launch. In 1999, a group of passionate creatives led by the agency BBH, came together to create the iconic "Keep Walking" tagline. This signature phrase travelled the globe for many years and single-handedly captured the spirit of the brand.

Now, I can keep going on and on; but to summarise, the power of creativity as a discipline in our craft is enormous. I feel grateful that as marketers, we are in the position to impact the lives of people with our work. Most importantly, you can and must utilise creativity as a discipline to build brands that stand the test of time.

So, do you feel convinced of the power of creativity? How will you embrace creativity in your daily life?

I would like to end off this communication with a quote which I find so apt for today's Friday email:

"Every science begins as philosophy and ends as art: It arises in hypothesis and flows into achievement."
—Will Durant, American historian and philosopher.

Cheers,

Siew Ting

SOUL INFUSION TIPS

- Find the aha! moment. Keep asking "why, why, why".
- Learn how to connect the dots.
- The recipe for creativity: Failure, daydreaming and failure first!

CHAPTER 12

Fostering Alignment and Courageous Leadership

*"If you want to walk fast, walk alone. If
you want to walk far, walk together."*
—African proverb

Dear Team,

One of the many charms of marketing is that you get to really test your skills in collaboration, stakeholder management and more. This includes your peers in the C-suite.

I first got to test these skills at a very early stage in my career. In my first role at Diageo, I was asked to lead a team of cross-functional team members across the globe, for the reinvention of a second whisky brand. The role required me to indirectly inspire my peers, who did not report to me, to develop a marketing mix of the second whisky brand, Windsor, in a very short and ambitious timeframe. I consider this experience as fantastic, as it helped me pick up stakeholder management skills at a peer level. This is one of the most important skills for a marketer or a CMO—to be like the director of an orchestra, but without the authority or direct hierarchy of power. How do you, then, stay connected and collaborate with your peers?

Peer-to-Peer Leadership: The Role of CMO as a Multi-stakeholder Leader

In June 2019, an article published by McKinsey & Company, entitled "Marketing's Moment is Now: The C-suite Partnership to Deliver on Growth", stated that the CMO's rapport with the C-suite is crucial in establishing the role of marketing as a growth driver. The data shows that 83 per cent of global CEOs say that marketing can be a major driver of growth. However, in this same survey, which interviewed the CMO's C-suite peers, only half of the CFOs surveyed said that marketing delivers on the promise of growth and 40 per cent did not believe that marketing investments should be protected during a downturn.

Moreover, their analysis showed that high-growth companies are seven times more likely to be a "Unifier CMO". According to the study, a Unifier CMO is someone who "fosters robust, collaborative partnership across the C-suite" and makes intentional investments to develop mutual benefits. These CMOs are also able to adopt the mindset of other C-suite executives to think in terms of an enterprise-wide strategy. They also invest time in clearly defining the role of marketing in the eyes of their C-suite colleagues.

Fostering Alignment and Collaboration

Perhaps the closest real-life experience I had of this was when I joined HP as the Asia-Pacific CMO. Armed with a newfound zest and excitement, and directed by advice from mentors and allies within the business, I was quick to realise that in order for me to earn a seat at the business table, I first needed to reposition the role of marketing within HP. This meant starting with the Asia-Pacific C-suite leadership team. I also understood that to be successful, I needed to collaborate with the CFO, the chief human resources officer (CHRO) and the chief technology officer (CTO). I started by engaging them early on with my hundred-day plan and vision for the marketing organisation. Then, I worked hard to not only build strong relationships, but also to create "mutually beneficial" accountabilities that will help them in their role ae time.

Let's look at a few examples to bring this to life. The CFO was tasked by the then president to look at reducing the push budget with more pull budget in the P&L. The president wanted to divest more budget towards demand creation and marketing as opposed to the sales force. I immediately jumped on this opportunity and struck an alliance with the CFO to set up a task force to develop a financial evaluation of the effectiveness and efficiency of marketing and sales. I applied my learnings and helped the CFO create a win-win situation with the boss.

Now, let's talk about my partnership with the CHRO. The CHRO had an intentional strategy to build our brand as the "employer of choice" of the younger Gen Z. I seized this opportunity to partner with the CHRO on building the employee brand narrative and create a marketing team to be part of the pilots for diverse and Gen Z networks. The CTO is responsible for providing faster turnaround of data to help create a better customer experience and faster generation of insights. I volunteered my team to lead the technology automation throughout the customer journey.

These are just a few examples of how I create mutually beneficial relationships. In the process of establishing these relationships, I also spent time forming an idea of what marketing really stands for and how it creates value for the leadership team and the corporation. It was an intentional strategy and journey to create the right relationship and foster the right alignment.

One may ask: In this example, was I armed with the right experience? Well, I doubt it. But I knew deep down that it was my role to create and foster the right relationship, so that I can position myself and gain credibility for marketing to be seen as a lever of growth.

Once I gained permission to do that, I needed to go into the second part of the plan, which was to execute what I have promised, to gain credibility.

Importance of Courageous Leadership

Now, fostering alignment and increasing collaboration with your peers—is this an easy path with no obstacles? Certainly not. It requires serious commitment and a willingness to understand different individuals, backgrounds and what makes them tick.

Leadership is an art and like any art, it requires a diverse palette of skills. Some of these may come naturally, perhaps ones like effective communication and the ability to inspire and motivate. An essential element of leadership that often doesn't come naturally is courage. In my journey of over 25 years in diverse leadership roles, I have come to appreciate the indispensable value of courage in leadership. True leadership, to me, is about charting unfamiliar territories and bravely confronting challenges. An article entitled "The World Needs Your Courageous Leadership", captures the essence of this sentiment well.

Courage is not an automatic response; it's a skill that can be cultivated. Being a courageous leader means defying instinctive reactions when confronted with uncertainty, ambiguity or tough decisions. It forms a cornerstone of leadership, laying the foundation for other vital leadership qualities, such as clarity of purpose, self-awareness, inclusivity and integrative thinking. From my tenure at multinationals, such as Unilever, Mars, and HP, I've witnessed how a company's trajectory can be significantly influenced by a leader's fortitude. Every choice we make, every strategy we implement, reflects our beliefs, our personal narratives and our courage to forge ahead despite the uncertainties.

Leaders today find themselves in a constantly evolving landscape marked by volatility, uncertainty, complexity and ambiguity, often collectively referred to as "VUCA". In these unpredictable conditions, courage empowers leaders to move forward. It enables them to make decisions when historical data is insufficient or unhelpful.

It's essential to recognise that humans are wired for fear, not courage. Common fears include the fear of failure, fear of looking foolish and the fear of damaging one's reputation. These fears often deter individuals from acting, paralysing them. Moreover, humans are biologically inclined to avoid losses, even if it means missing out on potential gains. These biases profoundly influence our decisions, often without us realising it. Understanding these biases and behaviour patterns is the first step towards transforming them. To become a courageous leader, you must confront your fears head-on and cultivate a new mindset.

Reading about the three pillars of a courageous mindset—embracing discomfort, risk, and failure—it struck me how often we, as leaders, shy away from these very aspects. But to truly evolve, to truly lead with purpose and impact, we must wholeheartedly accept these facets of leadership. It's a sentiment that I've tried to embody throughout my career, be it in bridging cultural nuances between the Asia-Pacific and the US or in advocating for an inclusive and diverse workspace.

Can Alignment and Collaboration be Learnt?

I certainly think they can be.

My first experience at Diageo showed that I was not naturally gifted with skills for collaboration and alignment. In fact, I had to unlearn my communication style to work towards alignment. Today, stakeholder alignment and peer collaboration are two of my "spikes", as shown in all leadership psychometric tests and feedback from my team. I certainly found a way to learn and practise it.

You may shudder at the thought of why the CMO C-suite role would be so challenging, but you must foster alignment and collaboration. I think this applies to all C-suite leadership roles as well. In fact, I feel that there is no better time than right now to be a CMO!

Have a fantastic weekend!

Cheers,
Siew Ting

S🌐UL INFUSION TIPS

1. Fostering a peer-to-peer relationship is an important lever to enable marketing to drive growth.
2. CMOs need to be comfortable with being a multi-stakeholder leader.
3. Fostering alignment and collaboration starts with a good relationship and intentional creation of mutually beneficial partnerships.
4. Getting your peers to understand the role of marketing and creating the right internal storytelling and positioning of marketing function's value is vital.

CHAPTER 13

Leading a Diverse Global Team: Global to Local, Local to Global

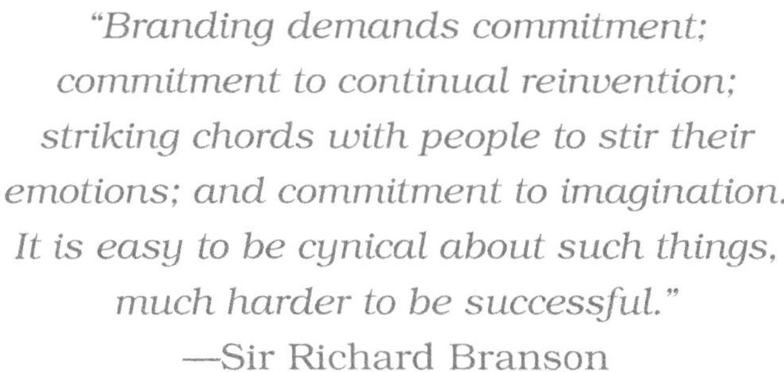

"Branding demands commitment;
commitment to continual reinvention;
striking chords with people to stir their
emotions; and commitment to imagination.
It is easy to be cynical about such things,
much harder to be successful."
—Sir Richard Branson

Dear Team,

Recently, I was involved in a panel where the moderator asked me what's my views on building a challenger spirit within global brands: What are some effective ways of leading global brands? Well, I have worked in five iconic global companies. Each one has a similar yet distinctly different global brand playbook and operating model. I don't think there is a magic route to reach it. The important thing, however, is context, and the macro environment that we operate in has changed and evolved, especially in the last few years.

As we begin 2024, the world continues to be in turmoil. We feel that time goes by too quickly, that technology is both a blessing and a curse, and that keeping track of all the internal and external forces that impact our lives (directly or indirectly) is a daunting task. I see this as us living in the world of the "unthinkable". With technology available at your fingertips, how should global brand leaders guide teams to build global brands with local soul? How do we implement the principle of "global to local, local to global"? How do we lead properly? How do we act as the protagonists and simultaneously, as the scriptwriters of the future of the brands we lead?

1. Start with purpose, then figure out the vision

In this age of uncertainty, people and organisations need to be anchored to a purpose. Global brand leaders need to know their mission and clearly define their brand's intentions. Purpose is the way to the moral compass and the North Star, and an indication of where and what to sacrifice, especially in this age of transparency. This purpose guides the global brand team (both local and global) in how to operate and figure out the vision and the plan.

2. Brands play a role in enhancing people's lives

Business and brands are no longer just about profit. They are also about enhancing people's lives across the multiple communities that the business serves. The focus should expand to include stakeholders beyond the shareholders. This expanded circle of influence needs to be addressed through integrated approaches that drive both the brands and business' financial well-being over time. To achieve this, global brand teams need to have a holistic worldview of the macro, societal, economic, political, consumer and technological trends. They need to develop brands that serve a universal human truth with a differentiated brand promise brought alive in a consistent, yet relevant manner across multicultural spaces and geographies.

3. Brand teams need to live in both global and local lives

Gone are the days when global brand teams operated on their own, as did the local teams—all the while, continuously fighting over their differences. Technological advancement has created a world where local teams can know what happens to a brand, in a global context, within the next hour, with a simple click. Instead of spending time talking about roles and responsibilities, brand teams need to understand the consumers' needs and solve problems that they face in their daily lives. This ensures that the brand and the products play a critical role in a problem-solving setting. They need to embrace technology, e.g., AI, partnering with their creativity and curious minds to dedicate time to this craft. With the unthinkable world that we now live in, there has never been a more relevant age to dedicate time to solving this problem for the brands you lead.

4. Operating model: Centralise decentralisation

With global becoming more global and local turning to be more local, having a centralised-decentralised operating model is the way to go. What do I mean by this? There needs to be clarity in the structure and operating model of the roles and responsibilities between the global and local. Moreover, there must be a clear definition on what needs to be centralised—global brand positioning, visual identity, global creative platform idea—and what needs to be decentralised—local insight, local media and engagement plan, local GTM and promotional ideas. This needs to then be partnered with a culture of inclusivity and openness for rapid communication for speed-to-market to meet the increasing demands.

5. Build a community of collaborators at the speed of communication

Great global brand stewardship requires what I call servant leadership. One needs to play different roles at different times. Imagine being the leader of the All Blacks rugby team: You serve as a leader, a coach, a cheerleader, a goalkeeper and even the executor. You need to know which role to play and when, especially when you are leading a team of multi-cultural and diverse brand managers. Being authentic to your purpose and leading from the front, to align the purposes of the brand and the team is a model that I often use to harness teamwork.

Embrace best practices, practise "lift and shift", and leverage scale. This is what I often mean by the power of community. Most importantly, the speed of communication—and transparent communication at that—becomes even more critical given the era in which we serve, all for the sake of building a brand with soul to serve the lives of the people and the communities that we cater to.

I am fortunate enough to have sat in global brand teams (or lead global brand communities) like Dove, Johnnie Walker, Anlene, Singleton of Glen Ord and HP. A successful global brand community is the one that demonstrates and operates on the principles mentioned above.

As Warren Buffet has said, "It takes 20 years to build a reputation and five minutes to ruin it. If you think about that, you'll do things differently."

This is what I mean by building a global brand with a local soul.

Cheers,
Siew Ting

SOUL INFUSION TIPS

1. Define a clear purpose and vision to guide global brand teams, aligning them towards a common goal.
2. Focus on enhancing lives beyond profit, prioritising the needs of all stakeholders and staying aware of global trends.
3. Establish clear roles and responsibilities, centralising certain aspects while decentralising others, supported by rapid communication for efficiency.

CHAPTER 14

The Power of Reframing

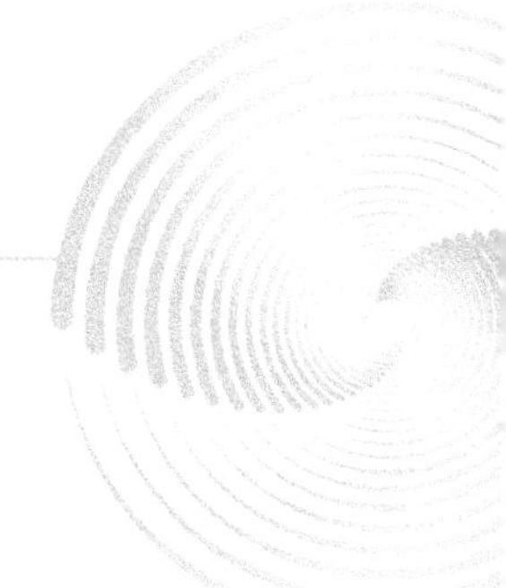

Dear Team,

Reframing is a superpower! Now, pay attention because I have something important to share with you this Friday morning.

When I was younger and inexperienced, if times were bad, then times were just bad; if times were good, then times were just good.

My ability to be happy or sad depended on everything going on around me. What people said or did (to me) had a massive influence on me because I sought external validation as the middle child.

As I grew older and wiser, and after receiving training from executive coaches, reading books, and going through many failures and disappointments, I learnt a real-life superpower: The power of reframing.

Without the superpower of reframing, we quickly slip back into a victim mindset. This mindset is one where we cede control of our power and relinquish our happiness and success to others. Why? Because it is someone doing something to us. We feel we have no agency. We feel powerless. This also trains us to blame others for our problems.

But when we reframe, we take back our power. We find beauty in the cracks. We find joy in the journey. We find meaning in the pursuit.

Let me give you a few examples of reframing from my life: I used to envy that as the Asia-Pacific CMO, me and my team did not receive sufficient investments for our brand, as we are in Asia and not the US. I know that Asia is a pocket full of gems, and now, we can start selling the role of each market—Japan for premiumisation, India for growth and Singapore for experimentation and aviation.

I used to begrudge that COVID had reset our world and we could no longer travel as frequently and so, I was not earning enough airplane miles. But now, I see its wonderful benefits. As opposed to spending weeks on flights, I turned all those hours into time that I can spend with my family and my little one. It is a gift of abundance.

I used to hate that I had to work insane, long hours. Past midnight, I would still be on the phone while the entire neighbourhood was fast asleep. Now, I count my blessings that I can fulfil my passion for marketing and create the impact that I want in global brand building.

I used to resent that I always inherited an insights team that had no travel budget for the past three years. The team had not yet physically met even after working together for so long. Now, I count my blessings that because we waited so long, our recent get-together demonstrated that rarity is precious and we can treasure these relationships and the moment even more.

I simply couldn't get my act together enough to exercise, even though I had all the means at my disposal, from signing up for a yoga membership to meditation practice. Now, after being truly present in a yoga retreat, I saw the fruits of daily practise. I reframed these moments of ritual as something one might do in a daily routine like brushing my teeth or enjoying a cup of coffee in the morning.

The following are two great, use cases of building a brand with soul, where I used the power of reframing:

Anlene

Female dairy nutrition, best known for its efficacy in preventing bone degeneration and mobility in middle-aged females.

However, there were several issues: Two years of declining sales due to lowered household penetration and no longer recruiting new consumers (though loyal users were super loyal).

Reframe: Focus on its strength-only female dairy nutrition brand, fronted by a powerful female brand ambassador.

She represents the generation of aging women who knows that age is just a number and they want to be able to be in their prime, regardless of age.

Boom! A series of product innovations, followed by a new repositioning brand campaign was launched.

Singleton of Glen Ord

Macallan is the first leading single-malt brand in Asia-Pacific. Its taste suits the Asian sensibilities. It is extremely smooth. The entire single malt Diageo portfolio was heavy and had a peaty taste, not suitable for the Asian palette. Diageo had an almost non-existent presence in Asia. The situation felt extremely bleak.

Reframe: Diageo owns 37 distilleries in Scotland, which sits on a wealth of single malt whisky. What if we create a single malt that is best suited to the Asian taste from scratch.

Bingo! The Singleton of Glen Ord Single Malt was created. To date, it is Diageo's best-selling single malt whisky in the world.

So, give me any situation and I will reframe it for you! Terrible situation? Reframe it.

Bad situation? Reframe it.

All of us have the superpower of reframing in us. We only need to take the effort to train that muscle.

Reframing is a superpower and it will set you free.

Resilience

I wrote about the fact that we are now living in the age of the unthinkable. Resilience is an important quality that current and aspiring CMOs must have. It is all about an ability to handle failure well and to bounce back. It is the ability to see each failure as an opportunity for progress and new creative ideas. This boils down to the individual mindset.

You guys might often hear me quote the Chinese term for crisis. The two characters "危机" mean "in every dangerous situation, there lies an opportunity". I see a crisis or a failure as an opportunity to reframe the situation or the narrative.

In the book *The Obstacle Is the Way* by Ryan Holiday, brought to life by the ideology of Stoicism and inspired by Marcus Aurelius, the author discusses the art of turning trials into triumphs. If you have not read it, I strongly recommend doing so. The book talks about mechanisms and actions to help achieve this transformation. As Aurelius rightly said, "The impediment to action advances action. What stands in the way becomes the way."

Give it a try. Let's flex that muscle of "reframing"!

Cheers,
Siew Ting

S☉UL INFUSION TIPS

1. Unlock your superpower: Reframing. Picture it—every challenge you face is like clay in your hands, waiting to be moulded into something beautiful. Reframing is that superpower that turns hardships into stepping stones and setbacks into opportunities. It's about finding that silver lining, the beauty in the cracks and joy in the journey.

2. Embrace your inner resilience: Hey, sometimes life throws you curveballs, eh? But guess what? You're tougher than you think. Resilience isn't just about bouncing back. It's about rising stronger. It's the grit that turns "I can't" into "watch me". It's seeing a failure, not as an end, but as a chance to rewrite your story—to grow and to thrive.

3. Live by Stoic wisdom: Practise seeing every obstacle as a secret door leading to a world of possibilities. That's the magic of Stoicism. It's about embracing the journey, finding wisdom in adversity and turning every stumble into a victory dance. So, when life throws you a curveball, channel your inner Stoic and turn that setback into your greatest comeback.

CHAPTER 15

The Learning Mindset

"What you think, you become.
What you feel, you attract.
What you imagine, you create."
—The Buddha

Dear Team,

The da Vinci CMO talks about the 10 experiences and five attitudes required to succeed. Through the years of trying, experimenting and learning, I believe that there is one additional attitude that underpins all these values: The learning mindset.

It's All About the Mindset

Are we all born with a particular mindset? Is it true that after a certain age, there are things that you just can't learn? I want to challenge the idea of a permanent mindset. Contrary to what people might believe, everything starts with the mindset, including whether one has a fixed or a growth mindset.

It has been repeatedly proven throughout the years of leading transformations, that the people in my team with a growth mindset are the most likely to succeed. They are great catalysts for change. In fact, truth be told, I look for people with a growth mindset to be on the bus I drive! A growth mindset is critical in building a brand with soul and forming marketing teams that help drive business growth. The mindset also determines your learning agility, your ability to innovate and your willingness to fail and bounce back.

So, is a mindset permanent? If you have not learnt a certain skill or failed at a skill, can you relearn it? I often hear people using this phrase, "It's not what happens to you, but how you react to it that matters." This was remarked by Greek Stoic philosopher, Epictetus.

I have led multiple teams across diverse transformations. Through all the trials and tribulations, I realised that the permanence of a mindset must be challenged. A fixed mindset can be challenged—it's just that it will take a bit longer, and perhaps more failures and experimentations to get there!

The Power of Learning

As I write this email, I know that I was not born a marketing wizard or a creative genius. What I realised is that high on my strengths is my zest for learning and picking up new skills—whether personal, professional or in leadership and marketing. In the first 15 years of my career, I was quite fortunate to have met many great mentors who helped me hone my craft in marketing. By observing them and practising their principles in the assignments and on-the-job training, I moulded my marketing skills. Over the last 10 years, through the same learning implementation, I have discovered that I must broaden my leadership skills and foster being an excellent CMO with on-the-job training, learning from my peers, situational learning and reverse mentoring learning. I have also learnt through my failures, big and small. Some of these failures were easier to recover from while others took me longer. But each one of them had a lesson to teach me. Perhaps that is the common feature.

The da Vinci Story

Imagine a young Leonardo da Vinci starting his apprenticeship at the age of 15 with master painter Andrea del Verrocchio. Did he start taking lessons in the subtleties of painting masterpieces right away? Not quite. He started out doing menial chores like setting up the canvases, cleaning the floor and mixing paint. It was after a few years that he was allowed to paint minor figures commissioned by Verrocchio's workshop. He was only allowed tasks like drawing a hand in one painting, painting some trees in the background in another and so on. Was this work dull and boring? Probably. But with each assignment, his confidence grew and he was given a larger role to play with every commission that followed, until he started to develop an original style and gained recognition for his own work. Today, we call this learning on the job.

If I applied this to my career journey, my first 15 years were all about moulding my skills and craft in marketing. This included multiple aspects across the marketing value chain, e.g., the craft of insights, advertising creation, marketing performance, brand building, etc., at different geographical focus and scale, and diverse businesses and brands. My last 10 years were all about broadening my marketing experience while improving my leadership skills to build my own signature brand.

Throughout this journey, did I start with a skill set that I already knew or learnt immediately? The answer is no. A great example of this would be digital marketing and the more recent AI transformation. Fifteen years ago, when Web3 and digital marketing started, I did not know anything about those. I picked it up by learning from an intern and with on-the-job training. Likewise, I am approaching AI as a beginner, with a child-like mindset to learn whatever I can and be as curious as possible.

Marketing is a most fascinating craft that intersperses with humanity and technology. Hence, applying a learning mindset is critical if you intend to climb up the corporate ladder.

Likewise with leadership, I was not born a multi-stakeholder or purposeful leader. I am just grateful that several years ago, HP gave me the opportunity to take on my first role as CMO for the Asia-Pacific region. Hence, I had a platform to learn on the job and put my ikigai framework to good use and practise the da Vinci CMO leadership principles. I haven't mastered them yet, but I am learning every day.

Taking Care of the Self and One's Energy

Now, the pursuit of this journey requires you to constantly take care of yourself and manage your energy so your heart, mind and body are aligned to go from constant striving and advance to the thriving zone. As a Type A personality, my area of development is energy. I don't like to take breaks and whilst I am relentless when it comes to many things, I find it hard to put meditation and exercise into my rituals. Recently through a mini retreat, I started experiencing the rewards of taking better care of myself. I realised that I could become a better leader who is more creative and more approachable. Each of these mini retreats is also a moment for me to introspect, and adapt and align myself to the situation. I realised that this way, I can be in the thriving zone more consistently. Now, I am starting small, putting the rituals into daily practise and aiming to achieve a good level of consistency.

I encourage each and every one of you to find your mini retreats, so that you can fill up your inner sanctuary. It will get you from the "strive" to the "thrive" zone.

In summary, to become a successful CMO, having a learning mindset is critical. It allows you to adapt and be agile.

Cheers,
Siew Ting

SOUL INFUSION TIPS

1. Stay curious, stay sharp: Keep learning like there's no tomorrow. Every lesson, every mentor, every failure—they all shape you into a better CMO.

2. Get your hands dirty, get ahead: Just like da Vinci, start small and grow big. Embrace every challenge; they're stepping stones to confidence and expertise.

3. Fuel your fire, fuel your success: Take care of yourself. Find your balance with quick breaks, workouts or mini retreats. When you're at your best, success follows suit.

CHAPTER 16

Leading Change Through Influence

"A leader's role is to raise people's aspirations for what they can become and to release their energies so they will try to get there."
—David Gergen

Dear Team,

During one of my skip level coaching sessions, a team member asked me: How can you influence your peers and those who do not report to you? What is your magic formula to influence people to change and transform? These questions set me reflecting as I started to have my coffee this morning.

First and foremost, the role of a marketing leader or CMO is one that is about driving change. You must be comfortable with leading from the front to drive change and be the orchestrator of people who do not have a direct reporting line to you. This, in other words, is to influence others.

Let's face it. Humans do not like change. We are creatures of habit. So, how do you drive change, especially those who are your peers and whom you do not have a hierarchical authority over?

Over the last eight years of leading multiple transformation journeys, I have tried and tested some approaches. I do not think they are conclusive, but I think some of them worked and helped me with leading change through influence.

1. Finding a window for change

I have learnt that finding a right time or window for change is half the battle won. Change is easier when the business is not doing well or facing a crisis. This implied that the "business as usual" or "usual way of doing things" will not work and creates a compelling burning platform for change. These types of windows are the best for driving transformation, and influence peers and teams to come along.

Now, what if the business is doing well or when there is no compelling reason to change? What do you do?

This is when you must really practise your "listen-decide-communicate" skills hard. Be prepared to walk the hallway, be at the pantry and be connected on the ground to understand and observe any underlying opportunities and seek out key problems behind the symptoms, and then find and create a window for change.

I once created a window for change by starting my 100-day plan into a new role with a stakeholder's interview and I let the team listen to the authentic feedback of the stakeholders, regarding their expectation of the team I was leading. I even created videos of the stakeholders' interview sessions so that it is from the "horses' mouth". This then creates a burning platform for change as it is easiest when it comes from the stakeholders you serve as compared to coming from the leader who wants the change and has a personal agenda vested.

2. Bite-size the issues, simplify the story

Humans do not like change. They also do not like to solve hard problems, especially if they are big, hairy and audacious.

I love challenges and I like to start with an ambitious mission and vision. One that is big, hairy and audacious. However, I learnt very quickly that when the goal seems far-fetched and difficult to attain, people will evade it and reject it. Not everyone is like me. Hence, I learnt that a good transformation leader needs to be able to "bite-size the issues". Break the problem statement and issues down into simple issues. Simplify the story and make it sound like it is attainable and the goals are easy to reach. Then, create an inspiring rally cry towards it.

3. Starting a movement: Find the right allies

In marketing, we have seen many brands practise their communication and advertising strategies with concepts, such as "starting a movement". I am a firm believer of using this approach. Why? It seems to work for me through trials and errors.

What does starting a movement entail?

Starting a movement often begins with the leader who creates a compelling vision and mission, and displays and demonstrates courage and bravery to be the first one to charge towards this vision. The vision or mission needs to also be purposeful and rooted in a compelling reason for the transformation or change, whether it is driven by external or internal factors. The vision needs to articulate clearly the opportunity and what the reward is if one will to join this movement.

It also requires a next ally, who demonstrates an equal amount of bravery and conviction to join this movement. In all the movements that I have initiated, I am always intentional about the ally who will join me and I will enlist this ally to be the first leader to join me in the movement.

Then, it is about publicly displaying the act or actions towards the pursuit of the mission. When people start seeing the rewards and success towards the mission, they will start to follow.

An example of starting a movement will be when I was the Asia-Pacific CMO. My first role in this company was to ensure that everyone in the business, including the marketing team, reframe ourselves to become the most trusted and innovative world class marketing team to drive short- and long-term growth. My ally is the China market team. This includes the allyship with the China managing director. With executions and success stories proven in China, everyone around us is starting to feel confident of our mission. We all know that success begets successes. Everyone will soon jump onto this bandwagon!

There is a well-publicised Ted Talk video entitled "Igniting a Movement" whereby it shows a shirtless guy starting to dance amongst a huge group of people in a big field. He was joined by his first ally, who demonstrated strong leadership behaviour. I strongly encourage all of you to watch that video as it teaches all the leadership skills on how to ignite a movement.

4. Telling a story of hope

Have you ever wondered why people like to watch sports matches and competitions? People especially enjoyed the moment when the winner emerges or the moment when the award was presented to the winner and how the winner speaks about his or her feelings and story of how he or she attained the win. This is because we like to hear stories of hope and especially one that emerges with victory after trials and tribulations. Hence, being a mastery of storytelling is extremely critical in the journey of influencing others. You need to intentionally—yes, the key word is "intentional"—share success stories and wins, and be able to paint the story of hope and optimism. This must happen at the start, during the journey and at the attainment of the goal. This will motivate people to come along with you on the journey.

5. The power of vulnerability

This tactic is used in a contentious way. Not everyone is comfortable with this. However, I find this extremely powerful and compelling, especially if this comes from the heart of the transformation leader. Demonstrating emotions and fears are often seen as weaknesses in the corporate world. However, I do beg to differ. People who are authentic and willing to call out their fears are the ones who are most confident of themselves.

My first trial of this as the Asia-Pacific CMO was during a team workshop, midway through the change journey. In a regional leadership workshop with my team, I exhibited my vulnerability, and shared my stories and my fears on the pursuit of our mission. Lo and behold, it immediately broke down barriers, created a safe zone for everyone to open up and drove collaboration. More people were willing to jump onto the bandwagon or the movement with the commitment of the hearts and minds.

Of course, I will suggest that you do this with authenticity and in a way that is true to your brand.

The CMO Journey is About Leading Teams Through Transformation

I hope by the time you read this, you will not put off by this note and start wondering if the pursuit of a CMO role is the right one for you. Leaders, as you ascend the corporate ladders, you need to learn the skill of leading through influence. Influence will come from above and below, with your teams and even your peers. Picking up these strategies and tactics to influence will be extremely critical for your success at senior leadership level and even more so for a CMO.

I was not born with amazing influencing skills. In fact, 15 years ago, I delivered results through sheer strong, individual contributor skills. I was ignorant of politics and how to influence peers. Therefore, leadership through influence and collaboration can be picked up if you are willing to put on a growth mindset, and test and learn.

What are your thoughts and do you have other strategies that you have tried to share?

Cheers,
Siew Ting

SOUL INFUSION TIPS

1. Find the right window for change.
2. Simplify complex issues so as to make goals attainable and easy to reach.
3. Start a movement by creating a compelling vision and mission. Enlist key allies to join the movement.
4. Master the art of storytelling by painting a picture of hope and optimism.
5. Demonstrate authenticity and vulnerability to build trust.

Afterword

We live in turbulent times. Yet, it is my sincere belief that there has never been a better time to be a marketer or a CMO. I hope you enjoyed reading this book and learning about some of my wins and battle scars. I certainly do not think I have perfected the craft of becoming a human-centric CMO, but I know I am working every day to get to a nine or 10 out of 10! I am still very much an athlete training for the Olympics.

To sum up, I think the qualities required to be a purposeful CMO who builds brands with a soul that stand the test of time, must start with knowing oneself. Know your purpose, what you want to contribute to the world and how you want to impact it. Marketers are in the best position to impact people and the communities they serve, other than, perhaps, C-suite leaders. We can apply the art and science of marketing to affect the world, the consumers we serve, and the brands and companies we represent.

We also need to understand that it is important to collaborate and work with multiple stakeholders—that's the nature of this role—and influence enterprise strategy through the voice of the customer; to lead from the front by reorienting the enterprise to adopt a customer-first mindset. We need to be able to train the muscle of self-reflection to learn how to adapt as the world we operate in changes rapidly due to technology, given that we deal with the human minds. We need to lead with confidence while demonstrating empathy and communicating with heart and mind to bring people along. Most importantly, we must build resilient and curious teams; creative teams that are constantly learning and innovating.

In this book, I have shared tips on how I bring people along to walk the walk. I have always learnt by doing and leading by example. I have actively tried to avoid a top-down hierarchical approach to leadership. To be a successful marketer and leader, you need to build internal brand ambassadors for the company you represent. You need to partner creatively with your peers and business teams and reframe the internal storytelling. I know for sure that the modern world needs purposeful leaders who know how to lead by collaborating with multiple stakeholders. They also need to be able to lead teams and bring out the best in them by creating a culture of risk-taking, innovating, creativity and willingness to fail, but learn fast!

Just as Howard Schultz said, a brand with soul is intangible. You cannot quantify it with numbers, but you can feel it in the employees, the customers they serve, how the product comes up, the logo, the semiotics of the brand and even the t-shirt that the staff wears. I see this the same way in how a CMO of a key "mothership" appears—you can feel it from how the brand shows up, how the teams speak of the brands and the products they serve, what the culture of the team is like, and the level of the passion and engagement of the team. It is an amalgamation and representation of the leadership and purpose of the CMO, and the collective spirit of the community that they lead.

This book is not meant to be conclusive, but rather, a starting point for ongoing dialogue and development within the marketing community. It reflects my commitment to the principle of abundance and reciprocity—by sharing knowledge, we expand our collective capacity for innovation and impact. I hope this mini playbook will inspire and equip aspiring CMOs with the courage and skills needed to lead in the creation of brands that not only drive profit, but make a profound impact on society as well.

By sharing these lessons from my journey and the insights gained from both successes and setbacks, I aim to contribute to the nurturing of future leaders who can continue to elevate the practice of marketing to new heights. Through this book, I seek to help others unleash their potential, guiding them on their path to becoming visionary leaders who can build and sustain brands with soul.

Acknowledgements

First of all, I'd like to thank my husband Chin Hon Fai and my daughter Kayla Chin. If not for their encouragement and belief in me, I would not even have the courage to write this book. My husband is the most patient, kindest and most supportive partner on earth. He empowered me to pursue my ambition of becoming a CMO and supported me in my many travels that I had to undertake while he was the anchor at home with Kayla.

I would like to thank all the key mentors and sponsors in the first two decades of my career. Because of the fact that you saw my potential, I am standing here with credibility to write this book. In particular mention are: Chris Hadzilias, Michael Mars, James Thompson, Gilbert Ghostine, Tim Parkinson, Vivek Rampal, Chan Chow Keong and Amphol Nirutnaphaphan.

I would like to give special thanks to Yap Cheng Guat (Cheng) and Lim Keng Teck, the early Scott Paper marketing leaders who developed the amazing internship programme for me. Without that experience, I would not have decided to pursue a career in marketing and brand management.

I also want to acknowledge Frank van den Driest and Marc de Swaan Arons who founded the Institute of

Real Growth. I had the fortunate opportunity of being a part of the Global 100 Top CMO cohort in 2021, which set the foundation of my pursuit of becoming a human-centric growth leader. Many thanks also to Frank for writing a gracious Foreword for this book.

Special thanks to Sophie Devonshire for supporting my book and penning a heartfelt praise.

I would like to thank Hanifa Ali, my lifelong coach turned friend. It is because of her that I believe in the power of coaching and also through the many sessions together, I formed and found my purpose.

To Shradha Biyani, my book coach, who has been a huge help on this journey of writing my first book, thank you.

To the many colleagues and friends in HP, it is because of the learnings and journey in HP that propelled me to become a multi-stakeholder CMO and which ultimately made me decide to write this book.

Finally, to the many people whom I have mentored, coached and led throughout my career, particularly in the last eight years: Working with you and guiding you has been an all-round learning experience which has led to the many stories that I have shared in this book. Because of all of you, I have learnt to become a better human-centric marketing and business leader.

About the Author

Foo Siew Ting is a marketing leader with 25 years of experience in multinational corporations, including Unilever, Mars, Diageo, Fonterra and HP. She has held roles, such as Global Chief Brand and Insights Officer, and multiple Asia-Pacific CMOs. Siew Ting has redefined marketing paradigms by infusing human-centric growth strategies into global brand narratives while maintaining local relevance. Her foresight in digital and e-commorece innovation, coupled with a deep commitment to data-driven insights, has led to groundbreaking initiatives that have set industry benchmarks. A champion of inclusive leadership, she has also cultivated diverse, high-performing teams, fostering a culture of creativity and innovation. Siew Ting has been recognised multiple times as one of Asia' Top 50 Most Influential & Purposeful CMOs. At work and beyond, she is committed to inspiring change, nurturing potential, and building a legacy of brands that contribute positively to society and the economy. Siew Ting lives in Singapore with her husband and daughter.